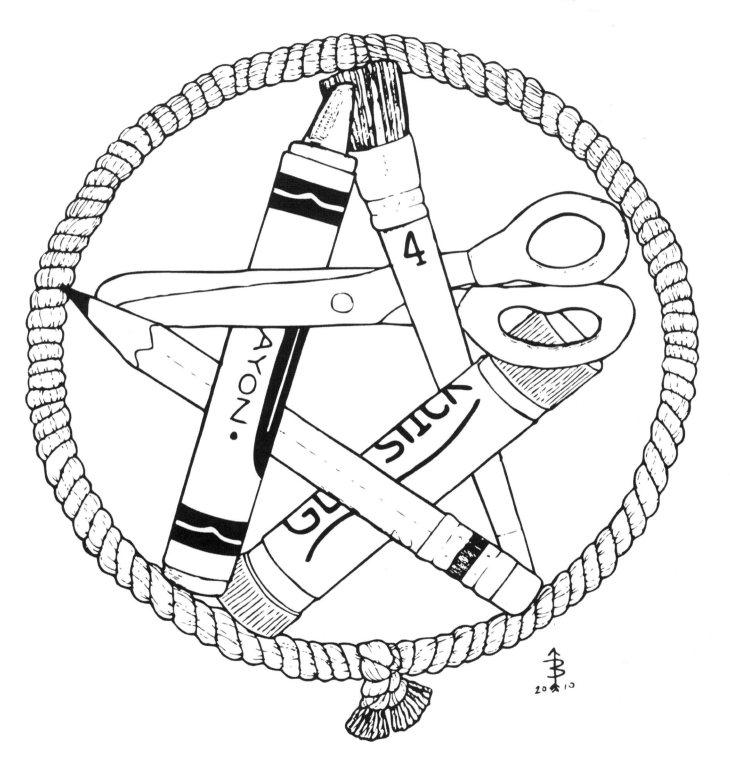

1

THE EARTH CHILD'S HANDBOOK

Book 2

The Seasons, The Sabbats & The Wheel of the Year

by Brigid Ashwood

The Earth Child's Handbook

Copyright © 2012 by Brigid Ashwood
Cover by: Brigid Ashwood

Website: http://www.earthchildshandbook.com
Featuring digital e-books, crafts, coloring pages, paper dolls, freebies and more.

Facebook: http://www.facebook.com/pages/The-Earth-Childs-Handbook/124662954255734

Twitter: https://twitter.com/PaganKidsBook

Contents

For Parents - How to use this book ……………......……… 7

For Kids - How to use this book ……………......……… 9

Chapter One - The Seasons, The Sabbats and The Wheel of the Year ………......…......……… 11

Chapter Two - Yule ……………......…... 21

Chapter Three - Imbolc ……………… 47

Chapter Four - Ostara ……………73

Chapter Five - Beltaine ……………......……… 97

Chapter Six - Midsummer ……………......…... 125

Chapter Seven - Lughnasadh ……………......……… 149

Chapter Eight - Mabon ……………......…... 171

Chapter Nine - Samhain ……………......……… 193

For Parents
How to use this book

I hope that this will be a book for your whole family to enjoy. While the bulk of the book is aimed directly at children - coloring pages, mazes etc are things they can do on their own; much of this book is intended for families and kids to participate in jointly. Most of the crafts and recipes are projects for several people, and the chapter introductions strive to give general background information on topics such as "why we honor the earth", and "what are the Sabbats."

I tried to give this book a broad base, to include many different Pagan ideas and traditions, and to keep the theme generalized, so that readers from very different paths might still find something valuable here. Since Pagan paths are so tremendously varied, this task was challenging.

Ultimately I chose an inclusive approach, drawing from many traditions and philosophies. I encourage you take from this book whatever fits your family and your beliefs. Discard what doesn't fit, and use this book as a tool to explore the beliefs of others with your children.

You may want to read the openings to each chapter together and discuss what you've read. How do your beliefs and family traditions resemble or differ from those in the chapter? Use this book as a jumping off point for a dialogue within your family.

I hope it serves you well.

Supplies

There are many crafts in this book that kids can do directly in the book, or cut out from the book and assemble. For these activities they will need limited supplies such as crayons, scissors, glue, glitter and double sided tape.

There are also other crafts and activities, which list supplies, and come with instructions. At the beginning of each craft I have offered a supply list. Generally substitutions can be made and I give suggestions where applicable. If a dowel rod is listed as needed, a stick from the backyard will generally suffice, use your imagination.

Consider keeping a craft box in a closet for a rainy day. I have provided a list of suggested supplies to try and keep on hand. This can be accumulated over time, and many of the supplies come from recycling, so get the kids involved in stocking the craft box. (This is also addressed in the Earth and Recycling Chapter)

Coloring Pages Etc

The coloring pages, mazes, word searches, connect the dots and other in book activities have all been printed with blank backsides. This is so you can rip the pages out of the book if you wish without fear of destroying any content that might have been on the other side.

Copies

Many of the cut out and assemble projects in this book (such as the Altar) will benefit from being printed on heavier weight paper. Please feel free to photocopy such projects on to heavy weight card stock.

Additionally, I know many families enjoy coloring pages repeatedly or have children vying for the same activity page. As an author of course I hope you purchase a copy of this book for every child in family. But I realize this is not realistic in many cases. Therefore, permission is granted for you to photocopy such pages for use within your individual family household.

Notes

Blank pages and added margin space in this book are by design. My hope is that you will make notes in the book, recording your own traditions, recipe adaptations, and ideas. Over time this book can become a personalized repository of family traditions and memories, perfect for being passed on to the next generation of 'Earth Children'.

Recipes

The recipes in this book are kept simple. Very few of them involve any complex preparation and many of them use pre-made store bought ingredients or packaged mixes. This was intentional to allow children the opportunity to do as much of the work themselves, as they can.

Many health food stores have packaged mixes that are tasty alternatives to some of the more mainstream prepackaged goods. And of course if you prefer to make a cake from scratch or use your own gelatin recipe this is great, the recipes will work fine with these substitutions.

Keep in mind age appropriateness and always be sure to assist the children when using the oven, stove, microwave or other potentially dangerous tool.

For Kids
How to use this book

This is a book full of magic and wonder, exploration and creation, crafts and activities, many questions, and hopefully some answers. Many of the questions you will answer yourself, others you will answer with the help of your family and friends, and always you will have fun doing it!

Being a Pagan means many things to many people. At times it can be confusing. Part of the aim of this book is to help you and your family better determine what being Pagan, means to you. As you do the crafts and activities in this book, enjoy spending time and crafting with your loved ones. Talk about the chapters and the activities; see what things you agree on and which things you don't. Above all have fun, and learn from your family.

The more you learn, the more you know, and the more you know the better able you are to determine your own beliefs and to appreciate the beliefs of others!

About the Crafts

You can read this book from front to back, or explore the chapters at your own pace. Any of the crafts and recipes can be adapted to work with other seasons. Just use your imagination.

Keep a craft box in your home and fill it with all the supplies you might need on a rainy day. Some you will have to buy, others you can recycle. Look around your home and use your creativity to find new uses for ordinary things.

Always keep safety in mind while doing these projects. Ask for an adult's permission or assistance whenever working with tools such as scissors or a hole punch. And when a project requires use of a stove or oven, make sure you have an adult available to do this part of the project for you.

While candles and fire can sometimes be a part of adult Pagan rituals it is not something for children to play with. Fire can be extremely dangerous and even deadly, always be sure you have an adult present to assist you if you wish to create a ritual with candles. There are plenty of candle-free alternatives in this book should you wish to do something creative on your own.

Above all have fun and if you don't have a particular supply for a craft project see if you can substitute something else.

Your craft box should contain:

scissors
hole punch
brass butterfly paper fasteners
white craft glue
glue stick
fabric glue
glitter glue
double stick tape
masking tape
craft paints (acrylic or tempera)
paint pens
puffy paints
glitter paints
fabric paints

crayons
colored pencils
markers
glitter
stickers
embellishments (charms, sequins, bells)
ribbon
string
yarn
shrink plastic
felt
fabric
flour
cornstarch
food coloring

dried herbs
stones
sticks
construction paper
newspaper
drawing paper
tracing paper
brown craft paper
paper towel rolls
toilet paper rolls
wrapping paper rolls
paper bags
plastic and glass containers
other recycled items

The Seasons, The Sabbats
and
The Wheel of the Year

Chapter One

The Seasons the Sabbats and the Wheel of the Year

Many Pagans these days celebrate eight holidays also called Sabbats. These eight Sabbats are spread throughout the 4 seasons and our calendar year. They are often referred to as "the Wheel of the Year". This is because as we walk through the seasons and their special days we walk through the cycle of life as seen on our planet.

We face the cold barren months of winter when the trees are without leaves and animals in hibernation.

We move on to the first glimpse of spring when the birds begin to tweet and the new buds are growing underground.

Then comes summer and the birth of baby animals, harvest of foods and long hot days full of our shining Sun.

With the final harvest we travel on to Fall with colorful leaves, crisp breezes, and preparation for the winter ahead.

As winter returns the wheel is complete, but has not ended, for we know that after winter the spring will return and the wheel begins anew.

It never ends, it is a constant cycle, just like the monthly cycle of the Moon and the daily and yearly cycle of the Sun, our Earth moves through her seasons.

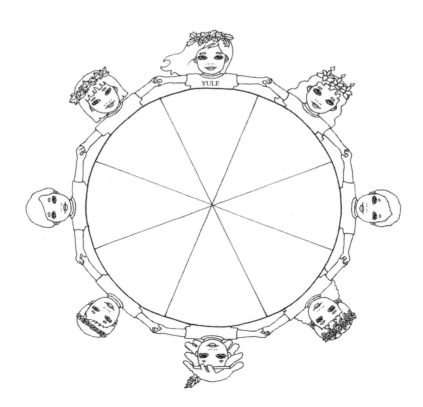

Seasonal Altar

Your family might want to consider having a family altar set up in a common room of your home for celebrating the seasons and the holidays.

We Pagans, with our eight holidays a year are very lucky, we never have to wait long for another exciting holiday season to be upon us.

As you travel through the Wheel of the Year with your family, you may find that you have your favorite holidays, you may find you celebrate some Sabbats more intensely than others.

However you celebrate, whether it be an all out occasion, or with just a few simple decorations and a special dessert, I hope you will consider the tradition of a seasonal altar.

To accomplish this simply set aside an area in your home that is frequented by everyone. Set up a small table and cover it with a cloth in a color or decoration appropriate to that holiday. On it set a bowl, and other items you might find to emphasize the Sabbat. Statues, candles, ribbon, branches, flowers, rocks, artwork etc, are all excellent choices.

You will also receive some suggestions as you read on through the Sabbats. In the bowl on the altar you might place something specific such as an offering of water or fruit to Spirit. (You can eat the fruit before it spoils or if you wish to leave the offering for Spirit, then dispose of it in a garden or compost heap before it spoils.)

You can also write wishes and prayers on slips of paper and tuck them into the offering bowl. On the night of the Sabbat have an adult burn the papers or bury them in a garden.

Above all....

HAVE FUN AS YOU CELEBRATE THE HOLIDAYS!

The Earth and The Sun

You can learn a lot about the meaning behind the Wheel of the Year, the Sabbats and the changing seasons from science and astronomy.

You probably already know that the Earth orbits the Sun. This orbit is shaped like a giant oval. So at some points during the Earth's journey it is very close the Sun, at other points it is very far away from the Sun. But the Earth's proximity to the Sun is not what causes the changing seasons. What causes the seasons is the rotation of the Earth as it travels its orbit. To see an example of this spin a dime on edge on a hard surface such as a large hardcover book. The dime spins around rapidly, but as it spins its body around, it also spins in an oval route across the surface of the book.

This is what the Earth does around the Sun, but with one difference. The Earth is tilted. Imagine that dime up in the air. It is spinning as it did across the book. But this time it has a line running down through the center of it. But that line doesn't sit straight up in down, it tilts off to the side, so that the dime itself looks tilted. This is much like the Earth's axis. As the Earth travels its orbit around the Sun it also revolves its body around the axis.

Every day the Earth makes one full rotation, providing us with our 24-hour day. Our Earth is a busy planet, it orbits the Sun and does daily rotations. At some times the top of the axis is tilted towards the Sun, at other times it is tilted away.

The part of the planet near the top of the axis is called the Northern Hemisphere. The part of the planet near the bottom of the axis is called the Southern Hemisphere. In between these two hemispheres is the Earth's equator. The equator is a belt around the middle of the planet showing it's exact middle. If the Northern Hemisphere above the equator is tilted toward the Sun, you can bet it is summer time in England and the United States. But if the Southern Hemisphere is tilted towards the Sun it is certainly summer in Australia.

So that means that different parts of our planet experience different seasons at different times. So a Pagan in Australia might celebrate the Summer Solstice while a Pagan in the USA would be celebrating the Winter Solstice. For this reason often times Pagans in the southern hemisphere will reverse the Wheel of the Year to better suit their environment.

Solstice & Equinox
Quarters

The Wheel of the Year has 4 quarters and four cross quarters. The Quarter Sabbats are determined by the position of the Sun in the sky relative to the Earth's equator. If you imagine the position of the Earth's equator projected onto the sky, you have what is called the Celestial Equator. Since these Sabbats are related to the activities of the Sun they are generally associated with Male energies and the God. The quarter Sabbats are:

☐   **The Winter Solstice -** The Sun is lowest below the Celestial Equator and we have the shortest day and hence the longest night.
> **Northern Hemisphere:** December 20-23
> **Southern Hemisphere:** June 20-23

☐   **The Spring Equinox -** The Sun crosses the Celestial Equator, and we have a day and night of equal length.
> **Northern Hemisphere:** March 20-23
> **Southern Hemisphere:** September 20-23

☐   **The Summer Solstice -** The Sun is highest above the Celestial Equator and we have the longest day and hence the shortest night.
> **Northern Hemisphere:** June 20-23
> **Southern Hemisphere:** December 20-23

☐   **The Autumnal Equinox -** The Sun crosses the Celestial Equator, and we again have a day and night of equal length.
> **Northern Hemisphere:** September 20-23
> **Southern Hemisphere:** March 20-23

Cross Quarters

The Cross Quarter Sabbats fall at midpoints between the Quarter Sabbats. These Sabbats are often thought of as the most important of the eight holidays of the year. Although all the Sabbats are important these Cross Quarter Sabbats mark the beginnings of the next season in the wheel, a time for people to pay particular attention to their surroundings and prepare for the upcoming months. This was especially important to our ancestors whose very survival in winter months depended on storing enough food for the coming season. The cross quarter Sabbats are:

- ☐ Imbolc: (February 2nd)
- ☐ Beltaine: (May 1st)
- ☐ Lughnasadh: (August 1st)
- ☐ Samhain: (October 31st)

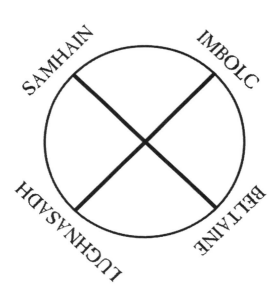

Note: Some Pagans celebrate their new year at Samhain, others at Yule. Either is a fine choice. Since the dates of the Sabbats can vary slightly from tradition to tradition and year to year, the dates given are approximate. In addition the dates for celebration are given for the Northern and Southern Hemispheres of the globe, as Pagans in the Southern Hemisphere may find it more appropriate to celebrate their holidays during the corresponding season.

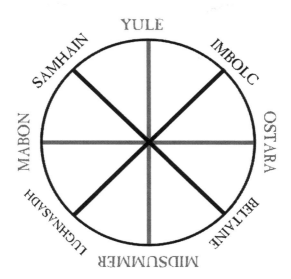

Together the Quarter Sabbats and Cross Quarter Sabbats complete the full Wheel of the Year. As we watch the seasons change around us and participate in the Sabbats we grow more aware of the world around us, of the life and beauty on our planet.

Another way to look at the wheel, rather then as just quarters and cross quarters is in sets of one, three, one, and three again. Yule and Midsummer stand alone as the holidays of our most extreme seasons; the dead of winter and the height of summer. While the remaining six holidays are often known as the three planting or fertility holidays of Imbolc, Ostara, and Beltaine; and the three harvest holidays of Lughnasadh, Mabon, and Samhain.

The Sabbats often feel like they don't belong to just one season. For instance Imbolc, which celebrates the awakening and coming Spring falls in February. But this sometimes-ambiguous nature of some of the holidays is probably a good thing; it keeps us looking ahead to the future instead of backwards to the past. We can feel the coming spring creeping up through the Earth at Imbolc and experience the urge to cheer on Mother Earth and lend her a hand if we can.

Maybe another reason for this is that many of our Pagan forebears didn't celebrate all eight holidays. Some ancients celebrated only the quarters, others only the cross quarters. Our modern Wheel of the Year has linked all of these Pagan holidays together to provide us with a year of discovery and celebration.

As you read through the Sabbat chapters you will find them broken up into seasons, keep in mind that this is just a learning tool and their placement is not written in stone. Another interesting thing is that each Sabbat on the Wheel has it's opposite. Trace the lines on the wheel to the opposite point and as you go through the holidays and learn about each Sabbat consider it's opposite point on the wheel and how they relate to each other.

Pronunciation Guide

Yule: YOOL

Imbolc: IM-bulk or IM-bulg

Ostara: oh-STAR-ah

Beltaine: BELL-tane or BAY-al-TIN-ah

Midsummer: Mid-summer

Lughnasadh: LU-na-sah

Mabon: MAH-bon or MAY-bon

Samhain: SAH-wen or SOW-when

Pagan Pals Wheel of the Year

Consider what you've learned about the Sabbats and the Wheel of the year.
Write the name of the Sabbat that goes with each child on the child's shirt. (Yule is done for you)
Then below each child write some of your favorite things about the Sabbat they belong to.
What are your favorite foods and activities from this Sabbat?
What fun facts have you learned about this Sabbat?
Don't forget to color and decorate the wheel!

Yule

Chapter Two

Winter – Yule

Other Names: Solstice Night, Yuletide, Alban Arthan, Saturnalia
Northern Hemisphere: December 20-23
Southern Hemisphere: June 20-23
Herbs: Clove, Evergreen, Holly, Mistletoe, Rosemary, Oak, Pinecones
Incense: Clove, Bayberry, Juniper, Rosemary, and Pine
Colors: Red, green, white, silver, gold, metallic colors
Decorations: Wreaths, garlands and sprigs of holly, evergreen, and mistletoe. Light strings and candles. Decorative trees, Yule log, strings of dried fruits and nuts. Apples and oranges stuck with cloves.
Foods: Dried fruits and nuts, poultry, hearty nut breads, spiced cider, dates, figs
Gods: Sun Child, Horus, Odin, Holly King, Jesus, Bel, Baldur
Goddesses: Great Mother, Isis, Lucina, Mary, Uarinna, Amaterasu, and Bast
Spirit: Rejuvenation, renewal, rebirth, rejoicing

Yule is the holiday of winter solstice. The Sun is below the Celestial Equator now and we have the shortest day and hence the longest night. After Solstice night the days will slowly get longer as the Sun climbs higher in the sky and stays out longer each day. Yule is celebrated as a holiday because it is considered the rebirth of the Sun God. We celebrate this time as a return of light and warmth into our lives. The Suns new light warms our frozen Earth and prepares her for the coming seasons of growth and fertility. This is a time of renewal and rejuvenation. Yule is is a festival of light and shares qualities with the holidays of other religions found at this same time of year such as Hanukah, Christmas, and Kwanzaa. All of these holidays recognize the principles of light, rebirth, and joyous expectation of the coming new year.

Yule Altar

Apples and oranges are representative of the Sun and with cloves inserted in a pattern around their skin are a fabulous looking and smelling decoration for your Yule altar.

Sprigs of evergreen twined about your altar and hung along the edge of the table is beautiful and fragrant as well.

Holly hung by the front door invites good fortune to your family.

Evergreen and mistletoe bring in the spirits of nature to celebrate the season.

Cinnamon sticks make lovely decorations. String popped popcorn and dried cranberries with needle and thread to make long garlands for draping about your home.

Red, green, silver and gold, sun prints, holly and evergreen prints, gold candles, and snowy glitter are all enchanting embellishments for your altar.

 If you wish to create a frosty look to the top of your altar sprinkle it with a bit of baking soda or flour to create a new "snowfall".

Yule Ritual

Often this time of year is associated with the practice of making resolutions. For instance you may wish to learn to play an instrument, or get rid of a bad habit in the coming months.

For this ritual you will need a small box and a bowl. The box you will decorate along with your family however you like. This will be your yearly Yule box and should reflect the themes of the holiday.

Have your family gather around a table. Place the box in the center of the table along with a bowl. Have everyone at the table write their resolution for the New Year on a slip of paper. Have each person place his or her resolution slip in the bowl. Pass the bowl around; each person will select a slip of paper from the bowl. Make sure you don't receive your own resolution. After the papers are passed out go around the table and have each person read the resolution on their slip of paper.

Everyone can take turns guessing whose resolution is on the slip of paper. Once they have guessed accurately write the name of the person on the slip, so you will be able to recall whose it is. Do this for each person present, and place all the slips of paper into the Yule box.

Everyone should resolve to not only work on their own resolution in the coming year, but to assist each other however they can. (This doesn't mean nagging your sister to stop chewing her hair, it means that if your Dad has resolved to give up candy bars, try not to eat them in front of him.)

After all the resolutions are read, write a family Yule letter. It doesn't have to be long, and in fact everyone can take turns adding a paragraph or two on their own. It should mention the significant events of the past year and any special feelings about this year's holiday.

Keep this letter and the resolution slips in the box and bring them out each Yule. Read over last year's letter before you write the current one, and check on those resolutions to see how successful they were!

The Yule Log

The Yule log is an old winter solstice tradition and often the highlight of solstice night. Traditionally the log was acquired off of your own property or received as a gift, you were not supposed to purchase your Yule log. Once a log was selected it was decorated with evergreen, holly and other seasonal green plants found on hand and placed in the fireplace.

It was then set to light with a piece of wood saved from last years Yule log. In this way the fire from this night was linked back to all those other fires that had gone before, all lit from a piece of wood saved from the previous year. Then the log was left to burn throughout the night and allowed to smolder for 12 days after.

On the twelfth night the ashes are dispersed outside to fertilize plants. If you have a fireplace in your home you and your family can create your own Yule log for celebration.

You can also create another kind of Yule log by having an adult drill holes for candles into the side of a log. You will want to slice off a bit of the other side of the log to enable it to lay flat. You may find something suitable as substitute in a gift or craft store to use, and barring all of these suggestions you can certainly make the Yule Log Cake recipe that follows! Yum!

Wassailing

Wassailing means to wish good health to. It is an old winter holiday tradition and was generally performed on the 12th night, the same night that the Yule Log burns out. Originally wassailing was an evening long event that included homemade apple cider or "wassail" and involved caroling and singing to local apple tree's to wish them good health and a good production in the coming year.

This custom evolved into general caroling and a wishing of good cheer and good healthy to family, friends and neighbors alike throughout the holiday season. Traditionally drums, bells and whistles were also used to wake up the tree and people often placed cider soaked pieces of bread onto the trees branches or lay them at its roots.

You might enjoy having a wassailing party during your Yuletide season. It is a great way to extend the cheer of the holiday. You might get a group of friends together at one person's home and carol around their neighborhood.

Or if you prefer to carol to your family and friends you can set out in early evening in one car and drive to each location for a few carols. This is particularly fun.

Dress warm, print off sheets of carol verses for everyone and inform the families on your caroling route that you will be coming. It is traditional for them to offer you a beverage and small snack as payment for your caroling. After an evening of singing and fun return to the home base and serve a light dinner with homemade wassail.

Wassail Recipe

2 quarts apple cider
¼ cup brown sugar
2 Cinnamon sticks (about 2-3 inches long each)
½ tsp whole cloves
½ tsp nutmeg
dash of orange zest
Piece of cheesecloth or clean white cotton cloth
String

Pour the cider into a large pan on the stove and set it to the lowest heat. Put all of the spices into the center of the piece of cloth, draw it up around the spices and tie it off with some string. Bring the cider to a boil and then allow it to simmer for 30 minutes. You can add a few pats of butter to the cider to produce a richer taste. Serve the cider in mugs with a cinnamon stick stirrer.

Yule Log Cake

This is a super simple recipe to make your own Yule Log Cake. Certainly you can make the cake and icing from scratch if you have a family recipe you would like to try, or you can use these store bought items to make a quick and delicious Yule Log cake with which to surprise your family.

Ingredients:
1 Packaged pound cake
1 container chocolate frosting
1 tube green decorative frosting
1 tube red decorative frosting
3 taper candles red, green, or gold, or any combination thereof

Set the pound cake on a serving plate. Slice off the top edges of the cake lengthwise and at an angle, you are trying to give the top of the cake a slightly rounded look like a log. Once you have achieved the desired loggy shape you can ice your cake completely with the chocolate icing. Use a spoon to dig out three little areas, space evenly apart across the top of the cake. Insert your taper candles into these holes make sure they are in securely.

Decorate the top of the cake and around the candles with the colored frosting. See if you can create holly leaves! Present your Yule Log cake at the beginning of your sabbat meal and allow it to serve as the table centerpiece while you eat.

Light the candles before you start eating so that they can burn down during the meal. When the candles are out, serve slices of your log!

Snowflake Ornament

Wide mouthed jar
3 white pipe cleaners
String
Scissors
Pencil
Boiling water (you will need an adult to handle this)
Spoon
Borax (called 20 Mule Team Borax Laundry Booster)
Blue food coloring (optional)

Cut your pipe cleaners into three equal lengths. Twist the three lengths together at their middles to create a six sided snowflake shape. If you wish to make a five pointed star shape simply cut off one of the ends and rearrange the other arms slightly.

Your snowflake should fit inside your wide mouthed jar. Tie a piece of string to the end of one of the snowflake arms. Tie the other end of the string to the center of your pencil. The length of the string should be long enough so that the snowflake hangs in the jar without resting on the bottom.

Have an adult fill the empty jar with boiling water. Add borax to the boiling water one tablespoon at a time. Stir it constantly to insure it is dissolving. Generally you will need to use about 3 tablespoons of borax per 1 cup of water. If there is some borax residue in the bottom of the jar, this is fine.

Now add the blue food coloring if you wish. Hang your snowflake in the jar so that the pencil is resting across the mouth of the jar. This will keep it from falling to the bottom of the jar and allow the crystals to grow evenly. The snowflake should be completely covered by the liquid but not resting on the bottom.

Allow your snowflake to soak in its jar overnight and you will discover it covered with crystals in the morning. You could decorate a whole tree for Yule with these ornaments or even give them as gifts. You can start a few months ahead of time and use recycled jars. Experiment with different sized ornaments, new colors and different shapes. Hang your ornaments in a window and watch them sparkle in the sunlight.

Note:
Borax can generally be found at most grocery stores, it can be hard to spot so you may need to ask for assistance. It goes by the name 20 Mule Team Borax Laundry Booster. There are other products on the market with similar names, but these are not the same chemical makeup and won't work in this project. If you are unable to find Borax, you may use sugar or salt in it's place, this is not ideal however and it will take considerably longer to grow the crystals on your ornament.

Cinnamon Solar cross ornaments

Make these delicious smelling ornaments to give as gifts for the Yule season. But don't eat them, they are just for smelling.

Materials:	Tools:	Embellishments:
1 1/2 cups ground Cinnamon	1 mixing bowl	Markers
1 cup Applesauce	Flat surface for kneading	Glitter
1/3 cup white craft glue	Wax paper	Craft Paints
Flour	Rolling pin	Puffy paints
Ribbon for hanging	Cookie cutters 1 circle and other assorted shapes	Foam stamps
	Drinking Straw	
	Empty ball point pen	

Mix together the cinnamon, applesauce and glue in a mixing bowl. Remove the mixture from the bowl and knead it on wax paper for several minutes until it has a firm clay consistency. Let it sit for about 30 minutes at room temperature to bind together a bit. Alternatively you can use a bit of flour when kneading the clay to cut down on the stickiness, it is then usable immediately.

Place a bit of clay between two sheets of wax paper and roll it out with the rolling pin. If the clay sticks to the wax paper you can dust it with a bit of cinnamon. The clay should be about 1/8 to ¼ inch thickness when you have rolled it out. Cut out a shape from the dough using the circle cookie cutter. Use the drinking straw to cut a small hole near the top of the circle. Don't cut it too near the edge or it won't be strong enough to hang up.

Now using the empty ball point pen draw a solar cross shape on the clay. Use the drawings of solar crosses below as your guide. It is simple a circle bisected by two perpendicular lines.

Make any other ornaments you like using the cookie cutter shapes. You can use cookie cutters or foam stamps to help you with designs. Place your ornaments on a sheet of wax paper and set them in a safe place where they can sit undisturbed to dry. The ornaments will take about 5-7 days to dry and you will need to turn them occasionally so that they dry nice and flat.

When they are dry you can paint and decorate your ornaments anyway you like. Thread a ribbon through the hole and tie it off to make a hanging loop. These ornaments make air fresheners especially for automobiles. They also make great gifts!

Yule Wrapping Paper

Make your own stamps from craft foam in various shapes and use them to decorate plain brown paper to make neat holiday wrapping paper. To make your own stamps you will need to make stamps bases from corrugated cardboard. A heavy cardboard box is a good recycled source for corrugated cardboard.

Cut the cardboard into squares large then the size you wish the stamp design to be. Stack several pieces of cardboard on top of each other and glue them together. This little cardboard "block" will become the stamp base. Draw your designs onto the craft foam and cut them out. Glue the designs to the cardboard blocks. Squeeze some craft paint onto a plastic plate.

Apply the paint to your stamp with a paintbrush (don't dip the stamp into the paint, you will get too much). Then stamp the design directly onto your paper. Press the stamp firmly and evenly all over before lifting it off the paper.

For your paper you can use brown paper grocery bags slit up the side, and with the bottom cut off so that they lie flat. You can also use rolls of brown packaging paper.

Holly Wreath

Make a Sabbat holly wreath. Cut the center out of a paper plate. Use a hole punch to make a hole in the top of the wreath, thread a piece of ribbon through the hole and tie it to make a hanging loop. Then use the holly templates on the next page to cut out green leaves and red berries from construction paper or felt. If you wish to draw the veins on the leaves you can do so with markers. Glue the leaves and berries all around the plate until you have your wreath looking full and complete. Hang it up and enjoy the decoration!

YULE
Word Search

Y	U	L	E	A	U	E	R	E	T	N	I	W
O	K	P	L	I	G	H	T	S	P	A	K	Y
P	M	E	C	T	E	B	A	K	S	X	B	A
D	C	I	G	F	O	P	D	R	T	R	E	E
R	A	N	S	Y	L	I	M	A	F	H	R	A
K	E	A	P	T	B	O	N	S	I	N	F	E
U	S	B	Y	U	L	E	L	O	G	C	S	R
Q	I	T	I	P	N	E	O	C	H	A	I	N
D	N	C	A	R	U	G	T	S	A	G	I	A
I	N	A	C	R	T	S	H	O	L	L	Y	P
E	B	R	S	G	L	H	A	I	E	W	E	X
S	O	L	S	T	I	C	E	G	C	A	P	E

YULE	TREE
MISTLETOE	STAR
HOLLY	WINTER
YULE LOG	SOLSTICE
GIFTS	REBIRTH
FAMILY	LIGHTS

NOTES

NOTES

NOTES

NOTES

NOTES

NOTES

NOTES

NOTES

Imbolc

Chapter Three

Winter/Spring – Imbolc

Other Names: Candlemas, Brigid's Day, Oimealg, Lupercus, Candlelaria, Disting
Northern Hemisphere: February 2
Southern Hemisphere: August 1-2
Herbs: Angelica, Basil, Bay Laurel, Blackberry, Heather, Iris, Violets, and first Spring wildflowers
Incense: Basil, Bay Laurel, Violet, Vanilla.
Colors: White, Pink, Red, Yellow, Spring Green.
Decorations: Wreaths of wildflowers, figures or artwork of ploughs (to symbolizing planting and fertility), brooms, Brigid's Cross, candles
Foods: Seeds and nuts, lemon poppy seed muffins, dairy products (soy dairy can be substituted.)
Gods: Young Sun God, Eros, Horned God
Goddesses: The Maiden, Persephone, Brigid, Innana, Gaia
Spirit: Purity, cleansing, growth, fertility

Although the Sabbat of Imbolc falls on a date when many parts of the world are still in the throes of a snowy cold winter, it is a holiday in celebration of Spring and the first fragile new buds of life that are emerging from the thawing ground. This Sabbat is generally associated with three themes; light, milk, and the first buds of Spring. Ancient people noticed that at this time of year their herd animals started lactating again in preparation for feeding their offspring, many had already given birth to new babies at this time. This event was seen as the first welcome sign that spring was indeed on its way. By this time the winter solstice has passed and the days are getting noticeably longer, in some areas the first few struggling plant buds can be seen peeking up through blankets of snow and fallen leaves.

Ancient Pagans celebrated this time with foods made with milk, by lighting candles to symbolize the returning lengthening days and by making crafts and engaging in activities to herald in and welcome the blossoming springtime. Often this holiday is closely associated with a Celtic Goddess called Brigid. Brigid is a fire goddess and keeper of light, protector of women in childbirth, and patron of creativity. Many people make ornaments called Brigid's Crosses on this day.

Imbolc was also a time of spring cleaning and many households would clean out the old to make way for the new at this time, often setting a broom by the front door as a symbol of housecleaning, both physical and spiritual.

Imbolc Altar

Your Imbolc altar should reflect the first hints of Spring that are starting to emerge outside. Use fresh colors like white, pink and spring green. Use wildflowers (or silk flowers from the craft store) on your altar. Candles and holiday lights are appropriate for this holiday. Decorate an empty (and clean) paper milk carton with symbols and colors of spring to act as a centerpiece for the altar. Fill a bowl with milk (cow or soy) and set some floating candles in it. Be sure to have an adult help you with candles and remember to pour out the milk before it spoils. Seeds are another excellent symbol of Imbolc. Glue unshelled sunflower seeds to a picture frame with white craft glue. Draw a picture of your favorite Maiden Goddess and put her in the frame. You can make another for the God as well.

Imbolc Ritual

For your Imbolc ritual take a hike outside in search of the early signs of Spring. See if you can detect any new buds on trees and plants in your area. Traditionally it has been considered "bad luck" to pick any new flowers or plants at this time. It is up to you to decide if you agree with this idea or not, but it is perhaps a wise notion to leave these fragile new plants alone and act in accordance with a "look, but don't touch" policy to insure their healthy future. You may enjoy getting a field guide for your area to take on your hike; it can help you to identify plants and wild life you find on the way. Most of all just enjoy the experience, say hello to the trees, breath in the fresh air and share some words of welcome with the waking Earth.

Imbolc Recipe – Pancakes

In some parts of Europe it is a tradition to make pancakes for your family on Imbolc.
1 cup flour (all purpose)
1 tbsp sugar
2 tsp. baking powder
1/4 tsp. salt
1 egg beaten
1 cup milk
2 tbsp vegetable oil

Combine all of the dry ingredients together in a bowl. In a separate bowl mix the egg, milk, and oil. Pour the egg mixture into the dry ingredients. Stir the batter well. It will look a little lumpy. Have an adult cook the pancakes in a lightly-greased skillet pan on the stove. This recipe makes about 8-10 regular sized pancakes. You can add other ingredients to the pancakes to liven them up if you like. Try adding a pinch of cinnamon, chocolate chips, cooked corn, or berries. But not all together! Yuck!

Brigid's Cross

A Brigid's Cross is traditionally made from wheat stalks and is a loosely woven designed that symbolizes the four elements, balance, fertility, prosperity and luck for the coming year. Often they were woven and given as gifts. Follow the instructions and pictures below to make your Brigid's Cross. You can use straw or reeds collected from outside (you may wish to soak them in water for a few hours to encourage them to bend rather then break as you weave) or you may find some straw at the craft store. If none of these items are available you can use pipe cleaners or thins strips of paper.

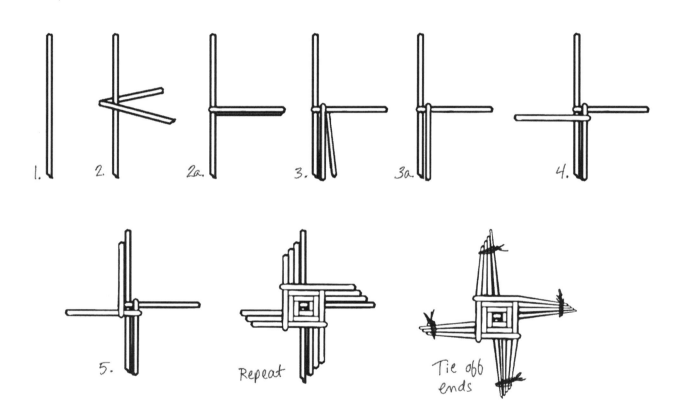

Bride's Bed

Since Imbolc is a holiday associated with the Maiden Goddess, young woman would often celebrate by making a doll's bed out of a basket and placing in it a doll in their imagined image of the Maiden Goddess. They would carry these Bride's Beds (Bride pronounced "breed" is another name for the Goddess Brigid) to neighbor's homes and ask for gifts for the maiden doll. This was seen as a symbol of good luck for the coming spring.

For this project you can use a doll of your own or one of the paper dolls from the front of this book. Fashion your doll a Sabbat outfit from paper, fabric, or felt. Decorate her dress with flowers and colors. To fashion her bed you can use a basket or decorate a small cardboard box. Use your imagination and have fun. Flowers, straw, lace, felt, glitter, sticks, acorns, seeds, and curls of ribbon are all lovely items to fancy up your doll's bed.

When she is done place her on your Sabbat altar. Traditionally Bride's Beds were made by young women and then carried from house to house in their village. Neighbors and friends bestowed small gifts upon the little doll and her maker. You can recreate this tradition in you own family by having an adult take you to the homes of your family and friends. You can also go from room to room in your home and have each family member present token gifts to the maiden.

Homemade Paper

Making homemade paper is a great way to celebrate Imbolc. Remember how we learned that Imbolc is considered a time of spring-cleaning, of getting rid of the old to make room for the new? Well making paper is a great way to recycle lots of paper trash and junk mail you might have in your home. It does involve a little bit of prep work and making and acquiring a few tools, but after your first time you be a pro. There are so many things to do with homemade paper. Stacks of homemade sheets and envelopes make great gifts. You can make special decorative papers to use in other crafts projects. You can make your own personalized stationary. You can use your own handmade paper to make paper clay. If you find that you and your family really enjoy this hobby then you may want to save up your junk mail throughout the year and separate it according to texture and color.

The kinds of paper that can be recycled for making hand made paper include:
Newspaper (grey paper)
Old unprinted computer paper (if printed the paper will be grey)
Magazines (makes a colored paper)
Old Cards (makes a heavyweight paper)
Paper Bags (makes a colored paper)
Egg Cartons (color of carton)
Tissue Paper (for translucent lightweight papers)
Construction Paper
Junk mail (this should be grouped roughly by color and separated into shiny and unshiny)

Materials:
Fiberglass Window Screening
Wooden picture frame
20 sheets of felt (available inexpensively from craft stores, preferably white.)
Liquid Starch (optional if you wish to be able to write easily on the paper)

Tools:
Large deep plastic container (large enough for the picture frame to fit into easily)
Staple Gun
Old towels
Sponge
Board (a cutting board or cookie sheet will do)
Blender (This is for making paper pulp, this blender should be a designated craft blender and not used for food. It certainly can be an inexpensive model from a discount store, it just has to shred the paper, and nothing fancy is required.)

Embellishments:
glitter
seeds
flower petals
confetti

NOTE:This is a family craft and should not be done unsupervised. An adult will need to make the paper frame (called a deckle) and operate the staple gun and blender. After this part of the project is done, the children can participate in the crafting of the paper itself.

Homemade Paper - continued

Instructions:

To make your paper frame or deckle you will need to stretch plastic window screening across a wooden picture frame. Stretch it tight and secure it to the sides with a staple gun. Secure one side and stretch and secure the opposite. Work your way around this way, stretching and securing the opposite sides until the screen is secured taught across the frame. (Note: the front of the deckle is the smooth side of the frame where the screen is covering it completely. The bottom of the deckle is the side where the frame itself is still exposed.)

On a flat work surface lay out your old towels. Set out the board you will use for pressing (this can be a wooden board, cutting board, or cookie sheet). Set out your felt squares

Select the paper you wish to use for your first batch. There are no rules here, but generally you will want to choose similar colors, textures and sheens. Rip up the paper into small pieces. Put the pieces in the blender filling it up about halfway. Fill the blender the rest of the way with warm water, leaving some space at the top, you don't want to overflow it.

Turn the blender on the lowest setting at first and gradually increase the speed until the paper pulp appears nicely pulverized. This generally takes under a minute. Check that there are no large chunks of paper in the blender. Fill your plastic container about halfway with water. Add about 3 blender loads of paper pulp (this depends on the size of your blender and the size of your container).

The more pulp you have in your plastic container the thicker your paper will be. Stir your mixture up. If you wish to be able to write easily on your paper you will need to add about 2 tablespoons of liquid starch at this time. This will keep the paper from soaking up too much ink when you write on it. Also add any special items to the pulp at this time.

Seeds, flower petals, crushed herbs, tiny bits of glitter, string etc all make lovely additions to the paper. Lower the deckle into the pulp and hold it level under the water (be sure you have it right side up otherwise it will be difficult to remove the paper from the frame).

Wiggle the deckle a little under the water and slowly draw it up to the surface, this is to even out the pulp on the surface of the frame. Let the water drain away from the paper. Look at the pulp on the screen, if it looks too thick take some pulp out of the tub, if it looks to thin put some more in. This is just based on experience and you will learn as you go.

When the water has drained away and the frame is no longer dripping you will transfer the paper to a felt square. Tilt the deckle against the felt square until one side of the paper sheet is touching the square, then ease it the rest of the way down so that it is laying face down on the felt piece. With the sponge, press against the back of the frame to extract the water from the sheet of paper. Wring out your sponge into the sink or a bowl or directly back into the pulp container.

Once you have soaked up the water you will hold onto the felt sheet and then gently peel back the frame.

The paper should remain on the felt sheet. This can take some practice, just keep at it till you get it right.

Repeat this process for each sheet of paper, stacking the sheets on top of each other. When you have done the last paper sheet place a final piece of felt on top of it. Use the board to press on top of the stacked sheets of paper. This is to remove the excess water from the sheets. This can be messy, so be glad you got those old towels out. After you have pressed the sheets gently peel them apart (leave them on the felt, just separate the felt pieces from each other.) Allow the paper to dry completely and when it has peel it off of the fabric. When dry your paper is ready to use.

Ideas:
Add herbs, dried flowers, seeds, glitter, and other small bits to the paper pulp (when it is in the pulp container, not the blender) to make decorative paper. Add colored construction paper, food coloring or a squeeze of craft paint to make colored paper. Use different textured fabrics as drying sheets to give the paper different textures. Place leaves or thin flat cardboard shapes onto the felt sheets before you transfer the paper sheet to the felt. The shape will be embossed on the paper when it is dry.

Plant your Paper! Add wildflower seeds to your paper. In the spring plant a sheet of paper in the ground. As the paper degrades the seeds will embed in the earth and flowers will grow!

This kind of paper makes a great gift! Write a letter to a loved one and send it in the mail. They can plant the letter and grow flowers that remind them of you.

Ritual: Write inspirational words on your wildflower seed paper. Write your hopes and dreams, and remembrances of loved ones. Plant the paper in the ground and literally watch your words and dreams thrive!

Hand rolled candles

Imbolc is a holiday often associated with light. In fact one old Imbolc tradition involves placing a single lit candle in the window of every room of your house. Many people like to carry on this tradition today (make sure you have the assistance of an adult, and never leave burning candles unattended). You can do this by using lots of real candles in your Imbolc celebration, or by stringing holiday lights around your house, or placing electric candles in your window. Another great way to celebrate is to make your own handmade candles. This is yet another craft that makes a great gift.

Materials:
Sheets of flat beeswax
various colors (available at
craft stores)
Candle wicking
Cookie cutters
Ribbon

Tools:
Cutting board
Pizza Cutter
Wax paper
Ruler
Masking Tape

To make stick candles:
The wick of your candle should be at least ½ inch longer then the length you wish your candle to be. So if you want to make a 8 inch candle you need 8 ½ inches of wick and a sheet of wax 8 inches wide. Don't worry too much about the length of the wax sheet as you can use several sheets to achieve the desired width of your candle. Tape a piece of wax paper down on your work surface. Use a pizza cutter and ruler to cut your wax sheet.

Starting with room temperature wax, lay your wax sheet down and place your candlewick against the end closest to you and lying widthwise to the wax. It should be flush against the edge of the wax sheet. Press the wick firmly into the wax. Begin rolling the wax sheet around the candlewick. Move your fingers up and down the length of the wick, pressing firmly and rolling tightly. The tighter your candle is rolled the longer it will burn later on. Roll the candle to the opposite edge of the wax taking care to roll the candle straight as you do so. Press the exposed edge into the candle to seal it and you are done.

You can experiment by cutting shapes from colored wax with cookie cutters and inserting the shapes between the layers of wax as you roll. You can also press colored wax shapes onto the outside of the candle to decorate it. Bundle several candles together and tie them with a ribbon to present it as a gift.

Imbolc Candle Crown

Make a crown of paper candles to wear on your head for this holiday of light. Cut at strip of paper long enough to fit around your head. Use the template below to cut a candlestick and flame from construction paper. Paste the flames to the candles and the completed candles to the crown itself. Embellish your crown with glitter, stickers and whatever else you like. Tape the two ends together, put the crown on your head and light up the room with your glow!

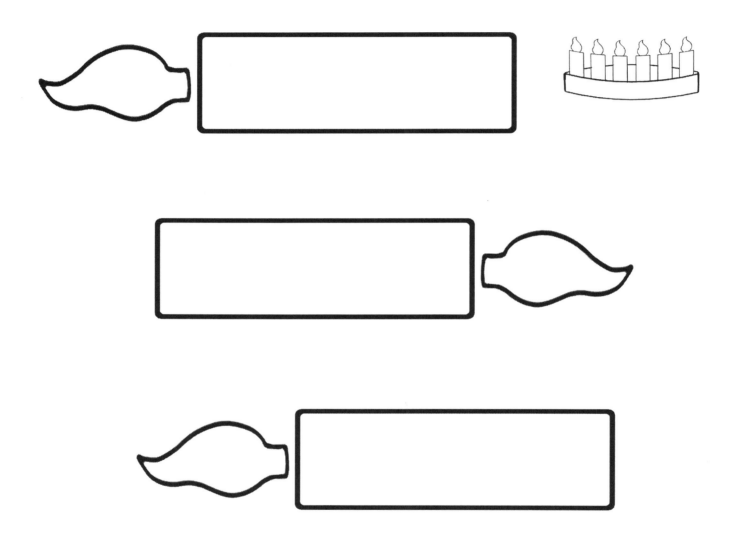

IMBOLC

IMBOLC
Word Search

G	C	R	O	W	N	O	F	L	I	G	H	T	O
B	R	I	G	I	D	G	U	S	T	J	L	C	B
A	R	O	C	A	N	D	L	E	S	L	I	A	N
G	P	I	U	E	F	M	A	U	C	S	G	N	E
N	F	Q	G	N	A	R	V	E	K	V	H	D	D
I	N	E	R	I	D	S	T	U	O	L	T	L	I
N	C	Q	B	E	D	H	R	P	S	P	I	E	A
E	T	K	R	R	S	C	O	A	I	N	S	M	M
K	X	G	T	E	U	B	R	G	B	A	O	A	N
A	E	X	E	C	S	A	P	O	D	P	V	S	R
W	S	T	B	G	O	I	R	T	S	A	S	Y	O
A	I	M	B	O	L	C	H	Y	K	S	Y	I	C

IMBOLC   CANDLEMAS
CORN MAIDEN   AWAKENING
LIGHT   MILK
CANDLES   GROUNDHOG DAY
BRIGID   BRIGID CROSS
FEBRUARY   CROWN OF LIGHT

NOTES

NOTES

NOTES

NOTES

NOTES

NOTES

NOTES

NOTES

Ostara

Chapter Four

Spring – Ostara

Other Names: Vernal Equinox, Spring Equinox, Alban Eiler, Lady Day
Northern Hemisphere: March 20-23
Southern Hemisphere: September 20-23
Herbs: Cherry Blossoms, Daffodil, Violet, Peony, Iris, Tulip, and other spring flowers
Incense: Jasmine, Rose, Strawberry, Violet, Vanilla.
Colors: Spring Green, Yellow, Pink, Lavender
Decorations: Decorated eggs, baskets, rabbit items, flowers, pastel colors
Foods: Green vegetables, hot cross buns, egg dishes
Gods: The Green Man
Goddesses: Eostre, The Maiden, Kore

Spirit: Birth, new life, hope, joy

Remember that the days have been getting longer and longer since the winter solstice, on this day they catch up with the nights and are exactly even. The Sun crosses the Celestial Equator, and we have a day and night of equal length.

Because of this the Vernal Equinox is also known as the first real day of spring. We may have more cold weather in some areas of our planet but at this point there is no denying that spring is definitely on its way.

Ostara has a lot in common with another holiday that occurs at this same time called Easter. It is a celebration of spring and new life popping up all over. Baby animals are being born and spring flowers are emerging, birds are chirping and some summer insects are buzzing around. Symbols for this holiday include eggs and rabbits which are popular symbols of life and fertility. The themes of purity, renewal, cleansing, and joyous expectation that we discovered in the previous Sabbats are present here as well. It is traditional to purchase new clothes at this time and open the windows in our homes to air out the doldrums of winter a bit.

Ostara Altar

The Ostara altar is full of color and life. When decorating this altar use lots of color. Spring colors such as light green, sky blue, pink and lavender are especially nice. Make paper garlands of colored construction paper to decorate your altar. Fill bowls full of decorated eggs (decorate plastic or wooden eggs so you don't have to worry about spoilage.) Shred colored paper and use it as filler for baskets full of fruit and muffins. Put white carnations in water colored with food coloring and watch them soak up the colors of the season. You could do pink for the Goddess and green for the God and place them in their proper places on your altar.

Ostara Ritual

Ostara Ritual and Spell - Wish Eggs

Ostara is a time of joy and happy expectation and is a great time to ask Spirit for special things to come to you. This ritual includes all of the four elements of earth and the fifth element of spirit. It is a ritual of balance and positive change. Ideally you will make the craft part of this ritual a few days before the Sabbat.

Ingredients:
1 Cup flour
1/2 Cup salt
3/4 Cup coffee grounds (preferably used)
1/4 Cup Ostara Herb Mixture*
1/4 Cup sand
1 cup water
1 pinch of fire ashes

If you don't have a fireplace to provide the ashes you can ask an adult to safely burn a piece of paper and include the ashes from this. Alternatively they can light a match, extinguish it and break off the match head to use in the mixture.

Ostara Herb Mixture

Lavender, Dogwood, Trefoil (Purple Clover), Honeysuckle, Thyme, Tarragon, Sunflower Seeds, Rose, and Dandelion. You can also add spring flowers and herbs native to your area. Mince the ingredients finely (you may need to wait for them to dry to do so) and stir together. You can use this mixture in craft projects, rituals and magickal workings to celebrate Spring! Don't worry if you don't have certain ingredients this mixture is meant to be personal.

Supplies:
Paper
Pen
Craft paints and brushes
Large Bowl
Spoon
Cookie sheet
Small gift items such as stone, semi-precious stones, charms, small toy etc.

Instructions:
On a small piece of paper write your desires for the coming spring. Do you want to learn to ride a bike? Does your family want to move to a larger home? Do you have a friend who needs cheering up? It can be whatever you want, something for yourself, for your family, for friends or the world, this is completely up to you. Concentrate on your wish as you write it down. Imagine that you are already riding that bike, living in that new home or that your friend is already happier. Roll up the piece of paper and set it aside. Think about your wish. Are there any herbs or stones that might complement your wish? For instance if you wished for happiness for your friend you might include a stone for healing such as rose quartz. Check the guide in the Ritual and Magick chapter of Book 1 of this series for assistance with these correspondences. Set the wish paper and other items to the side for now.

NOTE: Check the Imbolc chapter for how to make homemade wildflower see paper. It is perfect for this ritual!

Combine all of the dry ingredients in a bowl and then add the water. Stir the ingredients until they combine to the consistency of bread dough. Pinch off an egg sized piece of dough. You can make your egg any size that will accommodate your gift item. Roll the dough into a ball, poke a hole with your fingers into one side of the ball, going about halfway in. Insert the rolled up paper with your wish, and any stones or herbs into the hole, lastly insert the small gift item. Breathe into the hole and concentrate on your wish. You can whisper what your wish is into the hole if you like.

Close the hole with more clay and shape the ball into an egg shape. You can let your egg air-dry for 2 to 3 days or until hard. After your egg is dry you can paint and decorate it. You might try including symbols on the outside of the egg such as runes or symbols of the God and Goddess. (Again check the Ritual and Magick chapter for references.) On Ostara evening take your wish egg outside to the base of a tree or other large plant and say these words:

Goddess of Spring and life anew - Guide me in this spell I do.
From this egg my wish will grow - and come to life - this I know!
Earth, Air, Wind and Fire - bring to me what I desire.
Goddess of Fertility - hear my call - so mote it be!

Smash the egg at the base of a tree. Remove your gift item and keep it in your room in a safe place such as your altar or special box. The smashed egg will recycle into the soil and help fertilize the surrounding plants.

By the way, did you find the four elements present in this spell? The herbs are Earth, the Water is water (of course), ashes represent fire and the words you whispered into the egg is air. Your final words before smashing the egg complete the spell with the element of Spirit.

Plant this Greeting Card!
(Requires craft instructions from Imbolc Chapter)

This is such a neat craft to make and send in the mail to your family and friends. To make this project you will use the instructions for paper making found in the Imbolc Sabbat Chapter of this book. When making the paper you will include seeds in the paper pulp so that the recipients of your cards will be able to plant them in their garden. When the cards biodegrade the seeds will germinate and soon they will have wildflowers.

To make this craft project you will need to purchase several packets of wildflower seeds from a local nursery or garden supply center. Remember that you will need a least a dozen or so seeds to make their way into each card so have an adult assist you with determining how many packets of seeds to buy. Dump the seeds into the paper pulp mixture in the plastic tub before you start making your paper sheets. Omit the liquid starch!

Follow the rest of the instructions from the Imbolc chapter and allow the paper sheets to dry.

Fold your handmade paper into cards. Decorate your cards, insert them into envelopes and mail them off to your friends! Be sure to tell your friends to plant their cards in their backyards!

Tissue Paper Flowers

Make these lovely tissue paper flowers to decorate your home in the colors of spring.

Tools and Supplies:
Assorted colors of tissue paper
Pipe cleaners
Scissors

Select several sheets of colored paper in various colors. You want at least 6 sheets, the more sheets you have the fuller your flower will be. Cut the sheets to the size you wish your flower to be. The size of a sheet of notebook paper (8 ½ x 11) is a good size to start with. Stack the sheets on top of each other. Position the sheets in front of you lengthwise (the shorter end facing you).

Fold the sheets over about 1 inch and crease the seam. Still holding the sheets turn them over and fold another inch back in the opposite direction. You are folding the paper sheets back in forth like a fan. Continue this until the entire length is folded. Pinch the sheets together in the middle and bend a piper cleaner around the middle. This will be the stem. Press the edges of the paper fan together and trim them a little. You can cut scallops, or fringe or points, whatever you like.

Lastly carefully peel up and fluff out each layer of tissue paper until your flower looks full and happy.

Scrap Fabric Wreath

This craft is a great way to recycle pieces of colorful fabric and it makes a fabulous colorful Spring wreath.

Tools and Supplies:
About 100 squares of assorted colorful fabric
Straw wreath
Paintbrush
Wire
Pinking shears

Use pinking shears the cut the squares of fabric. The pieces should be about 3-4 inches square. You will need at least a hundred to start, maybe more depending on the size of your wreath. Have an adult fashion a hanging hook on the back of the wreath with a piece of wire.

If the wreath is covered in plastic you can leave the plastic on. Take a piece of fabric and position it on the wreath, using the non-bristle end of the paintbrush push firmly in the center of the fabric pushing it down into the wreath. The fabric should now be stuck securely in the straw wreath.

Repeat this step inserting squares of fabric closely next to each other until the whole front of the wreath is covered.

Hang your wreath on the wall and enjoy!

Pysanky Eggs

Pysanky is a traditional Ukrainian craft of decorating eggs with wax and dye. The true Pysanky craft involves certain tools and techniques, our version is very simplified. If you find that you enjoy this craft you and your family may want to try the traditional version, you can find books on the topic and you may even look for classes in your area.

For this craft you will need a dozen hardboiled eggs, a white crayon, and assorted eggs dyes.

Draw a design on your egg with the white crayon, then dip the egg into the dye. Where the crayon has covered the egg the dye will not penetrate and your design will show through.

Experiment with different designs and dipping only portions of the egg into the dye at a time.

Ostara Recipe – Equinox Brownies

Hot cross buns are an Ostara tradition. They are sweet pastry rolls with a equal armed cross cut in the top and coated with frosting. You can sometimes find easy to make packages of hot cross bun mix at grocery stores this time of year.

An alternative to Hot Cross Buns is Equinox brownies. These brownies have chocolate chips to symbolize the dark of night, and white chocolate chips to symbolize the light of day.

1 package brownie mix
1 package chocolate chips
1 package white chocolate chips

Make the brownies according to the instructions on the box. Simple add 1 cup each of chocolate chips & white chocolate chips to the mix. If you have used a small box of brownie mix you may want to reduce this to ½ cup of each. Mix all the ingredients together and pour them in a lightly-greased pan. Spread it evenly. Bake in the oven for half the recommended time on the box. Check the brownies to see if they are done. They tend to bake quicker with all these extra goodies. If they are not done continue baking checking every five minutes so they don't burn. Of course have an adult assist you with the oven.

OSTARA

OSTARA
Word Search

N	E	W	L	I	F	E	B	C	A	M	H
Q	S	P	R	I	N	G	E	L	M	B	P
A	E	W	L	O	D	H	A	T	F	B	O
X	E	Q	U	I	N	O	X	E	U	Y	H
A	B	A	S	K	E	T	P	N	R	K	O
T	R	X	R	A	G	B	N	E	A	U	E
K	H	A	C	A	G	Y	D	P	J	D	M
C	Q	P	T	S	R	E	W	O	L	F	O
I	P	E	R	S	C	P	E	I	A	K	A
H	O	T	C	R	O	S	S	B	U	N	S
C	S	E	V	A	E	L	N	E	E	R	G

SPRING   BUNNY

EQUINOX   CHICK

FLOWERS   HOT CROSS BUNS

BEES   NEW LIFE

BASKET   OSTARA

EGG   GREEN LEAVES

NOTES

NOTES

NOTES

NOTES

NOTES

NOTES

NOTES

NOTES

Beltaine

Chapter Five

Spring/Summer - Beltaine

Other Names: May Day, Bealtaine, Beltane, Walpurgisnacht, Roodmas
Northern Hemisphere: March 21
Southern Hemisphere: October 31-November 1
Herbs: Almond, Bluebell, Daisy, Dogwoods, Cherry Blossoms, Honeysuckle, Hawthorn, All flowers
Incense: almond, Honeysuckle, Frankincense, Lilac, Rose, Wisteria, Vanilla.
Colors: Red, White, Green, Light Green, Lemon Yellow, Pale Pink, Sky Blue, Lavender
Decorations: Maypoles, ribbons, flower chains, beads, hearts
Foods: Red fruits, cherries, strawberries, cran-grape juice, Beltaine barley cakes, green salads
Gods: May King, Jack-in-the-green, Green Man, Pan, Faunus, Horned God, Dionyosis
Goddesses: May Queen, The Maiden, Flora, Diana, Venus, Aphrodite
Spirit: Love, friendship, romantic love, joyous celebration

It was probably at a fabulous Beltaine party a long long time ago that the term "party animal" was first heard. Beltaine was the ancient Pagan's way of relaxing and de-stressing after a hard long winter. They drank wine, and made cakes, they danced and sang, they wore flowers in their hair and beautiful new clothes. They played games and wove ribbons through their hair. They dressed up in fancy costumes and wore masks and acted out plays. What fun! Beltaine is a celebration of life and happiness. Frolicking and playing outside is especially enjoyable now that spring is fully underway and Summer is following close behind. Beltaine is a time to show your family and friends how much you love them, to make yourself an colorful new magickal vest, to leave surprise gifts of flowers on the doorsteps of your neighbors and play games, eat, drink and be merry!

Beltaine Altar

The Beltaine altar is one of flowers, flowers, and more flowers! Twist sheets of paper into cones, secure them with tape or staples and attach a ribbon handle to the top. Fill these cones with flowers and hang them on doorknobs or picture hooks in your home. You can surprise friends and family with these little paper vases as well. Make chains of wildflowers by tying the stems in loops, insert the next flower through the loop and tying it and so on. You can also use one long piece of ribbon and tie it around one stem at a time, then hang the whole garland across your altar table. Bright colors are wonderful now, and the green foliage of spring is especially vibrant. Pick some leaves and use them to line a plate or bowl. Float flowers in bowls of water. Braid three different colors of ribbon together to make a garland.

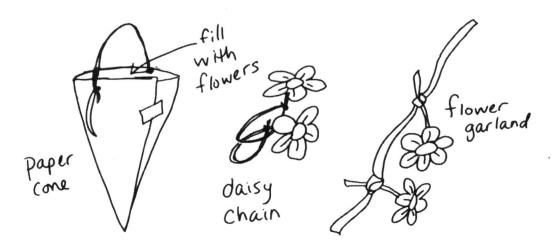

Beltaine Ritual - May Pole

A beautiful Beltaine tradition is that of dancing around a maypole. A maypole is a tall wooden pole planted in the ground. Attached to the top of the pole are long colorful ribbons, traditionally red and white, that reach all the way to the ground. The top of the pole is decorated with a wreath or arrangement of beautiful fresh spring flowers. Men, women, boys and girls all dance around the pole each holding a ribbon, as they dance they wind their ribbons around the pole. A maypole is kind of like a giant magic wand stuck in the Earth, by dancing around it, singing, laughing and weaving the ribbons we are charging it with energy. When we finish the dance and complete the weave we send our thoughts, energy and magickal light down through the pole into the Earth and up into the air and into the universe. Wow! What an amazing way to express your joy and what a powerful way to work your magick! If your family is especially crafty and handy with tools you can make your own full size maypole. You can do so with a large piece of lumber that is secured into a hole in the ground, and with ribbons nailed or stapled to the top. The craft below is an easy one that anyone can make without the use of power tools or lumber.

Supplies:
Empty wrapping paper roll
Hole Punch
Assorted colors of ribbon (4-6 feet in length, traditional colors are red and white)

Punch three to six holes in one end of the wrapping paper tube. Punch them a few inches down from the end of the tube so that they are strong and won't rip out when the ribbons are attached. Thread the ribbons through the holes and knot the inside ends. These knots will lie inside the tube and hold the ribbon in place. If you wish you can paint and decorate the remainder of the pole. It is that simple!

To use your maypole have the tallest person of your group stand in the middle of an open area, you need enough room to dance and run around. This person will become the maypole and they will stand in the center of everyone holding the maypole above their heads. The ribbons should trail down their body. Each ribbon dancer grabs and ribbon and starts skipping in the same direction around the pole. To create the weave you can have every other dancer skip in the opposite direction while also weaving in and out, to the left and right, of the dancers they encounter. While you dance you can play your favorite music or sing your favorite songs. It doesn't matter what you sing, the point is to have fun. You could sing something as simple as:

A-maying, a-maying, here we go a-maying
A-maying, a-maying, watch us dance and sing!

Once you have wrapped your maypole person completely in ribbons, everyone should hug that person at the same time give a cheer, something like "Yeah Beltaine!" or "Welcome Spring, Come on Summer". Do a few cartwheels and stomp your feet, make a ruckus and get silly, and don't forget to unwind your maypole person, be sure to give them a cupcake and some grape juice! If you find you enjoy maypole dancing you can find more information about building traditional maypoles, and specific traditional songs and dances in books at your library, bookstore, and online.

Beltaine Recipe – Almond Cherry Oatmeal Cupcakes

This is a simple and delicious Beltaine Oatcake recipe. It also includes other Beltaine foods such as red fruit in the cherry and almonds. Make this dessert as cupcakes and top them with little maypoles. You can make the maypoles from toothpicks and colored paper or ribbon. Cut three small strips of paper or ribbon and glue them to the top of the toothpick. When they are dry insert them in the cupcake and you are ready to go!

Topping
1/4 cup oats (quick cook)
2 tablespoons all-purpose flour
2 tablespoons brown sugar firmly packed
1 tablespoon cold margarine or butter
1/4 cup sliced almonds

Cake
1 package of yellow cake mix

Additional Supplies
1 can of cherry pie filling
Cupcake tin
Cupcake paper liners

Make the cake according to the instructions on the package. Ask an adult for assistance if you need it. Have an adult preheat the oven to the recommended setting on the cake mix. Line your cupcake tins with paper baking cups. Divide the cake batter up amongst the papers cups. Fill each cup up about halfway. Drop a large spoonful of cherry pie filling into each cupcake cup.

In a mixing bowl mix together the dry ingredients for the topping. Save the almonds for last. Then cut the cold margarine or butter into cubes. Drop the margarine a little at a time into the dry topping mixture. Mix the topping lightly by rubbing the butter between your fingers. You don't want the topping to be creamy, rather it should be crumbly with large chunks of butter and the other ingredients. Stir in the almonds. Sprinkle a healthy portion of topping onto each cupcake. Bake the cupcakes for about 5-10 minutes and then check them by poking a toothpick into the top of the cupcake from the side angled towards the center. You want to avoid poking through any cherry filling as this won't give you an accurate indication if the cupcake is done or not. Have an adult help you whenever you are dealing with the oven and hot or dangerous tools. Since oven temperatures vary you will need to determine for yourself when the cupcakes are baked completely. The toothpick should come out clean or with a slight bit of cake sticking to it, not with wet batter. Pop your toothpick maypole decoration in the top of these cupcakes and they are ready to serve.

Flower Beads Necklace

You can make clay with flower petals and use it to make beads for necklaces, bracelets or make a small decorative dish or other craft.

Recipe:
½ cup flour
1 tbsp salt
2 tbsp water
3 cups dried crushed flower petals (rose petals or lavender are good choices.)

You can crush the flower petals finely by making sure they are very dry and pouring them into a brown paper bag. Close the bag and then crush the petals through the bag.

Mix all of the dry ingredients together and add the water a little at a time while stirring. You may find you need a bit more or a bit less. Add water until the clay is the consistency of dry bread dough. You want it not to dry, but not to sticky.

Roll the clay into little balls and use toothpicks to poke holes to make beads. Allow the clay to dry thoroughly, this can take a few days, and then you can string the beads on string or dental floss.

You may prefer not to paint any crafts made with this clay as it will cover the flower petal texture. Experiment enhancing this clay with a few drops of food coloring, infused floral oils or essential oils.

Make a Beltaine Vest

Make a Beltaine party vest from felt and fabric. Have an adult help you with this project.

Tools and Supplies:
Brown craft paper
Felt
Fabric paints
fabric glue
ribbon
scissors
paintbrush
magic marker

To make the pattern for the vest, lay chest up on a large piece of craft paper. Have a friend trace around your shoulders, under your arms, and down your sides to your waist. Connect the spaces where your neck, arms and waist were. Add an inch all the way around the vest and you have your pattern.

Cut two pieces felt from your pattern. Lay them against each other and line them up so they match. With the scissors cut small slits in the fabric, about an inch from the edge. Do this across the tops of the shoulders and down the sides of the vest. Use the ribbon to lace the vest together at the tops of the shoulders and down the sides. Be sure not to lace up the armholes or the hole for your neck!

Now lay your vest down flat on your work surface and smooth it out. Cut a straight cut right up the middle of the front of the vest to create the chest opening. Decorate your vest with fabric paints. Cut out flowers and leaves, bugs, and butterflies from pieces of colored felt. Attach these to your vest with fabric glue. Lastly you can fold down the top corners of the front of the vest to create lapels.

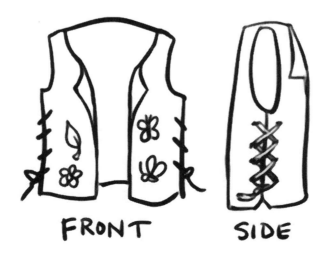

FRONT   SIDE

Beltaine Parade

Have a fabulous musical parade to celebrate the holiday. Make instruments from recycled items around your house.

Drum:
Have an adult punch a hole on either side of a coffee can with a hammer and nail. Thread ribbon through each hole and knot. Put the plastic lid back in place and hang the ribbon around your neck. Use spoons to bang on your drum.

Cymbals:
Bang together the lids to two pots! Add a little ribbon the handles to decorate.

Castanets:
Have an adult punch two holes in the lids of two jars. Thread ribbon through the holes and knot it together. Insert your index and middle finger through the ribbon of one castanet, and your thumb through the other, if the ribbon is too loose tie it shorter. Bang the two lids together between your thumb and forefingers.

Tambourine:
Tape or staple together two paper plates. Punch holes around the perimeter and attach bells (available at craft stores) tied with ribbon to the holes.

Shaker plate:
Put a handful of beans or rice onto a paper plate. Cover it with another paper plate turned upside down, and tape the plates together. Tape the entire perimeter of the plates so nothing falls out.

Guitar:
Cut a 3-5 inch circle out of the lid of a shoebox. Place the lid back on the shoebox and stretch several rubber bands around the entire box and lid lengthwise, being sure the rubber bands cross over the hole. Tape a ruler or stick to the back of the box for a handle.

Horn:
Make a loud horn to amplify your voice. Just decorate an empty paper towel roll. Hold it against your mouth and speak into it, your voice will be louder and carry farther.

Banner:
No parade is complete without a banner. Make a banner from scrap fabric, paper, or felt and ribbons. Attach it to the end of a stick, wooden dowel, or broom handle. Carry your Beltaine banner proudly at the head of the parade.

When you've finished making your instruments, gather some friends and family members and start your merry Beltaine parade! Dance around the living room, play your instruments and celebrate spring!

BELTAINE

BELTAINE

BELTAINE
Word Search

M	S	A	F	W	E	N	I	A	T	L	E	B
A	A	K	N	U	C	S	M	O	K	P	T	H
Y	E	Y	I	A	N	M	E	E	T	E	H	A
P	Q	I	D	C	A	P	R	A	U	E	J	S
O	C	X	B	A	D	N	C	Q	S	N	F	E
L	B	P	A	K	Y	S	U	C	T	I	C	D
E	G	U	I	E	F	O	P	D	R	O	P	N
S	K	H	R	I	B	B	O	N	S	I	N	A
U	G	L	O	V	E	O	A	G	I	A	T	L
E	B	R	S	W	E	X	T	P	N	C	S	R
E	C	T	E	B	C	A	P	E	G	H	R	A
D	A	I	S	Y	C	H	A	I	N	S	X	G

MAY DAY   BOUQUET

BELTAINE   DAISY CHAIN

MAYPOLE   GARLAND

DANCE   ROSES

RIBBONS   SING

CAKE   LOVE

Color the mask and decorate it as you wish. Cut out the mask along the bold black line. Cut out the eye holes. Punch out the side holes. Fasten string through the side holes and tie the mask around your head.

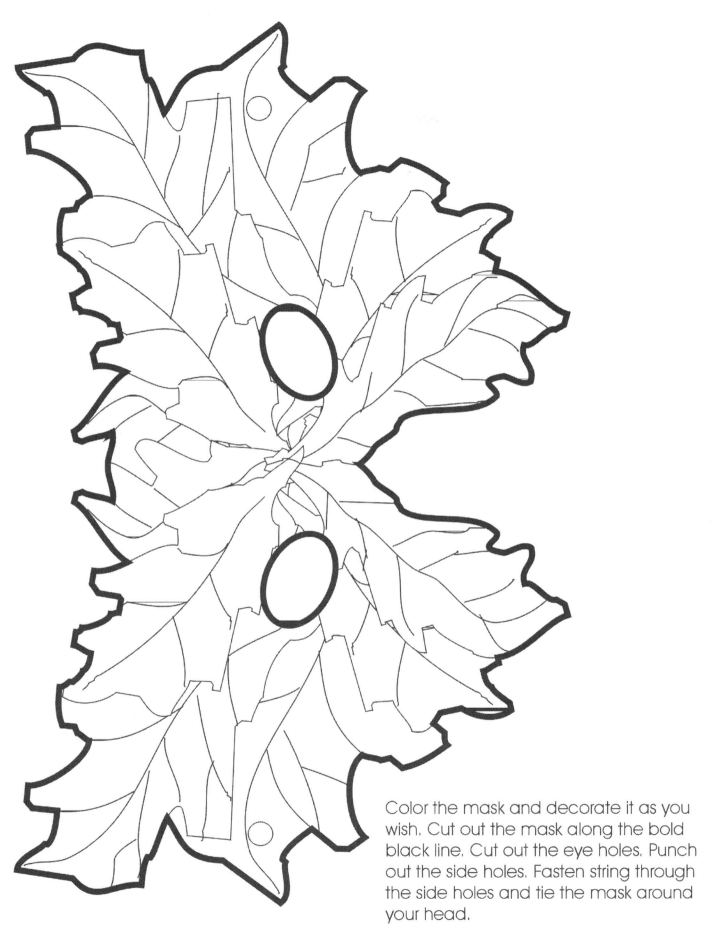

Color the mask and decorate it as you wish. Cut out the mask along the bold black line. Cut out the eye holes. Punch out the side holes. Fasten string through the side holes and tie the mask around your head.

115

NOTES

NOTES

NOTES

NOTES

NOTES

NOTES

NOTES

NOTES

Midsummer
Chapter Six

Summer – Midsummer

Other Names: Litha, Summer Solstice, Midsummer, Alban Hefin
Northern Hemisphere: June 20-23
Southern Hemisphere: December 20-23
Herbs: Chamomile, Bergamot, Rose, Lily, Oak, Lavender, Heather, Honeysuckle, Ivy, Yarrow, Fern, Elder, Daisy, Carnation, Dandelion, St. John's Wort.
Incense: Lemon, orange, bergamot, Myrrh, Rose, Wisteria, tangerine
Colors: Gold, Yellow, orange, peach, lime, lemon yellow
Decorations: Solar cross, flowers, sun symbols, fairies, seashells, sand, dried herbs
Foods: citrus fruits, vegetables, sorbet, lemonade, watermelon, berries
Gods: The Father, Father Sun, Pan, Cernunnos, Lugh, Balder, Ra, Apollo
Goddesses: The Mother, Mother Earth, Litha, Vivian, Cerridwen, Ishtar, Astarte, Aphrodite, Yemaya, Oshun, Aine, Freya.
Spirit: Dedication to Spirit, protection, purification, getting rid of negative energy and celebrating summer at the height of its glory.

Midsummer is the holiday of summer solstice. The Sun is at its highest above Celestial Equator now and we have the longest day and hence the shortest night. After summer solstice the days will slowly get shorter as we gradually head into fall and eventually winter. At summer solstice the Sun and The God are at the height of their power, the days are hot and long, plants and flowers are flourishing and people are enjoying the outdoors.

Midsummer is a great time to take a walk outside and see if you can spot some fairies, leave them a gift of cookies or juice and see if you can find some in a bush or under a shady tree. If you do this at dawn you have the best chance of spotting a fairy.

Another midsummer tradition is that of bathing in a stream or river, the running water cleanses your body and purifies your spirit, taking all the negativity away with it as it runs downstream. Of course you should always have an adult present if you are playing near water. So be sure to do this activity with a an adult guardian.

An alternative to bathing in a river is to take a dip in a pool or run around under a sprinkler and visualize becoming completely clean from the inside out!

Midsummer Altar

Your Midsummer altar should glow like the sun. Cover it with crisp yellows and metallic golds. Draw pictures of the sun, butterflies, ladybugs, bees, seashells and other symbols of summertime. Use seashells to hold small amounts of water and a single flower. Spread a little sand over your altar and draw symbols in the sand.

Make a textured sand painting with sandpaper and craft paints or crayons: Simply draw or paint directly on the sand paper.)

Make an underwater summer scene for celebrating Midsummer. Pour a little sand in the bottom of a clear glass bowl and fill it the rest of the way with water. Add seashells and floating candles.

Midsummer Ritual - Magickal SandPainting

Many cultures including Tibetan and Navajo have spiritual and magickal traditions involving the creation of art, and more specifically the creation of art using sand. A sand painting can be a powerful tool and exercise in meditation, visualization, ritual and even spellwork. This activity is meant to be done with the whole family with a common goal in mind. You will first make your own colored sand, then decide collectively on a purpose for the painting and the spell. You may decide to concentrate the energy on a working for just one member of the family or on something for the family as a whole. It is up to you. Before you do the painting research symbols that may be appropriate to include in your painting and for your spell. For instance if you wish to create a protection spell for a loved one taking a long trip you may look up a specific rune for protection and travel and incorporate it into your painting. You will need to prepare the sand a few days in advance of this ritual as it will need time to dry.

Colored Sand - Tools and Supplies:

Sand (you want what is labeled as play sand, found at craft and hardware stores, aquarium sand will work as well.)
Food Coloring
Assorted plastic containers
Paper towels
Plastic baggies

Instructions:
Use one bowl for each color of sand you wish to make. Fill ¾ up with sand; fill it with water until the sand is covered. Add food coloring to the water and sand and stir it. Allow the sand to sit overnight or until the sand appears the color you would like it to be. Carefully dump the water out of the container (you may wish to do this outside to avoid dumping any sand down the sink.) Scoop the sand out onto paper towels, spread it around a little and allow it to dry. Once it is dry you can store it in plastic baggies.

To Make the Painting:
Set a cookie sheet in the middle of a table. You can decide on a preset design for your painting and trace it on paper if you like, or you can allow each artist to just improvise their own design. If you are using a design then place the pattern on the cookie sheet. To distribute the sand you can clip off a very tiny corner of the plastic baggies and allow the sand to flow out while you direct it, or you can put the sand in plastic cups and use spoons to apply it to the painting.

Think about the purpose of your spell while you make the picture, visual the positive outcome. Talk about this with your family and enjoy the creative process. When you have finished the painting link hands with your family and say a few final words about the purpose of the painting. This is the time to take a picture of the painting if you wish to be able to remember it, for the final step in this process is to destroy the painting. Have every family member place a hand in the cookie sheet and move your fingers around and across the painting to mingle the colors and designs. (Do not blow on your sand painting to destroy it as you may get sand in your eyes.) You can pour the sand from the painting and store it in a jar. Keep the jar in a safe place and don't attempt to reuse it for another spell.

If you did the spell for an individual you might wish to give the jar to them for safekeeping.

Midsummer Recipe - Fruit Salad

Fruit salad is not only delicious but super easy to make.

Tools and Supplies:
Large bowl
Spoon
Knife
Cutting board
Sugar (or honey)
Lemon Juice

Assorted fruits:
banana, grapes, strawberries, blackberries, raspberries, cantaloupe, watermelon, honeydew, oranges, tangerines, apple and whatever else you like

Wash, pit, peel and slice the fruit into bite sized pieces. Have an adult assist you with using the knife and cutting board. Mix all of the fruit together in a large bowl. Taste the fruit salad; if some of the berries are tart you may need to add a bit of sugar to sweeten it up. Add a squeeze of lemon juice to help keep the fruits from browning in the air too soon. Serve your delicious summer fruit salad. (A dollop of whip cream or ice cream might go nicely with fruit salad too!)

Solar Cross Wreath

The Solar Cross is an old symbol used to depict the Sun. Make a Solar Cross wreath from a circle of cardboard and glitter.

Tools and supplies:
Cardboard
Scissors
White craft glue
Gold orange yellow and red glitter
Ribbon

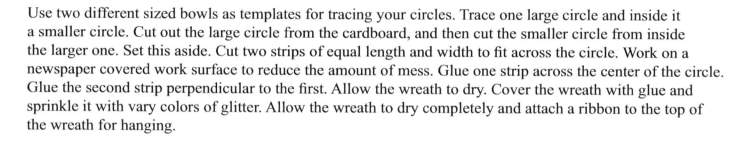

Use two different sized bowls as templates for tracing your circles. Trace one large circle and inside it a smaller circle. Cut out the large circle from the cardboard, and then cut the smaller circle from inside the larger one. Set this aside. Cut two strips of equal length and width to fit across the circle. Work on a newspaper covered work surface to reduce the amount of mess. Glue one strip across the center of the circle. Glue the second strip perpendicular to the first. Allow the wreath to dry. Cover the wreath with glue and sprinkle it with vary colors of glitter. Allow the wreath to dry completely and attach a ribbon to the top of the wreath for hanging.

Sand Clay

Making this clay involves the use of the stove, so you will need an adult to assist you.

Tools and Supplies:
1 cup sand (play sand, or aquarium sand)
1 1/2 teaspoons powdered alum (spice section of the grocery store)
1/2 cup corn starch
1/2 cup water

An old saucepan.
Foil lined cookie sheet

Mix together all ingredients in an old saucepan. Heat the mixture over medium heat, stirring constantly. The mixture will liquefy somewhat, and slowly start to thicken. Keep stirring about 3 minutes until mixture is thickened. Remove the pan from the heat and spread the clay onto the foil lined cookie sheet to cool. Once cool your sand clay is ready to use.

This is great clay to use in making decorative rock like pieces with carved symbols. You can press seashells into the clay to make fossil like impressions and even use it to model yourself a permanent sandcastle.

Store unused clay in an airtight container.

Pressed Flowers

Summer's bouquet has such diverse variety of flowers why not preserve them to use in crafts and enjoy them year round. Go on nature walks with your family and collect wildflowers. Press the flowers in an old phone book. You don't need any fancy flower press, but you may need several old heavy phone books if you really enjoy this craft!

Allow the flowers to sit in the phone book for a few weeks to dry and flatten. You can label the pages with post notes and allow them to stick out the edge of the phone book so that you can easily find which flowers are where in the book. It's now a flower directory!

Use white glue thinned with a little water to paint glue onto your pressed flowers and apply them to paper craft projects such as stationary, gift cards, decorative candles (not for burning), picture frames, place mats, bookmarks and whatever else you can dream up.

Arrange an assortment of flowers on a piece of paper to make a pressed bouquet and frame it as a gift. You can protect flowers on cards, place mats and bookmarks by covering them with a piece of clear contact paper or packaging tape. For very tiny flowers you can use tweezers to pick them up and arrange them on the paper.

Summer Time Straw Buddies

Color the strawbuddy.
Cut it out.
Cut slits at the dotted lines.
Slip a drinking straw thru the slits.
Now you have a strawbuddy to help you enjoy
your favorite cold summertime drink!

MIDSUMMER

136

MIDSUMMER
Word Search

M	P	E	S	L	I	E	C	I	T	S	L	O	S
L	I	T	H	A	V	E	K	V	L	C	H	Y	E
S	C	D	A	P	O	E	D	H	R	N	O	F	A
U	N	W	S	T	A	R	F	I	S	H	B	R	S
N	I	O	R	U	N	C	Q	B	A	I	E	A	I
S	C	T	L	I	M	K	S	Y	N	K	R	E	D
H	G	P	W	A	R	M	C	B	D	J	N	D	E
I	T	B	G	O	I	M	E	A	S	Y	O	I	B
N	C	G	N	I	N	E	D	R	A	G	R	S	E
E	G	T	U	O	L	A	E	X	N	F	Q	T	B
G	B	A	C	P	S	D	K	X	G	E	C	U	M
R	O	S	E	S	O	A	I	U	C	S	G	O	A

MIDSUMMER   SOLSTICE
LITHA   SAND
WARM   ROSES
PICNIC   SUNSHINE
SEASIDE   GARDENING
STARFISH   OUTSIDE

NOTES

NOTES

NOTES

NOTES

NOTES

NOTES

NOTES

NOTES

Lughnasadh

Chapter Seven

Summer/Fall – Lughnasadh

Other Names: Lammas, First Harvest, Apple Harvest. Lammastide
Northern Hemisphere: July 31/August 1-2
Southern Hemisphere: February 2
Herbs: goldenrod, peony, clover blossom, yarrow, Queen Anne's lace, rose, sunflower, poppy, mushroom, wheat, corn, rye, oat, barley, rice, garlic, onion, basil, mint, raspberry leaf, strawberry leaf, hops, grape vine
Incense: Rose, sandalwood, cinnamon, apple
Colors: Gold, Yellow, orange, rust, brown, dark green
Decorations: Braided Corn dollies, corn cob dolls,
Foods: apples, grains, breads, berries
Gods: Lugh, John Barleycorn, Grain God
Goddesses: Ceres, Demeter, the Corn Mother
Spirit: Prosperity, bounty, thankfulness, charity and compassion

The Celtic name of this Sabbat, Lughnasadh, comes from its association with the Irish Sun God Lugh. Some Celtic traditions connect this day with Lugh and the death of his foster mother Taillte. When she passed away Lugh held funeral games in her honor.

Other traditions associate this Sabbat with grain goddesses such as Ceres and Demeter, while the god is represented by grain gods such as John Barleycorn This is also a day associated with the harvests of apples and berries.

The theme of this Sabbat is most definitely harvest and bounty, and an awareness of the upcoming winter months. Food storage began, and people celebrated and gave thanks for the beginnings of a good harvest. Lughnasadh, or Lammastide, was also a time of craft fairs, music concerts, and stage plays, in fact the events and activities probably were precursors to our modern day craft and agricultural fairs, as well as Renaissance Festivals.

You might celebrate Lughnasadh with your family with a day of craft making and bread baking. Stage a short play, or have a parade, participate in games and enjoy the outdoors.

Lughnasadh Altar

The Lughnasadh altar is a merging of the colors of summer with the colors of fall. Oranges, yellow, peach, and pink, sit next to rust, brown, and gold. Braided wheat decorations and dried corncobs join bowls of apples. Braid lengths of colorful ribbon or raffia and drape them over your altar.

Have an adult cut the middle out of a few apples, insert votive candles or tea light in the hole and light the candle. Tie together three ears of dried corn to make a simple corn dollie for your altar. The three ears of corn represent the three aspects of the Goddess.

Lughnasadh Ritual – Herbed Bread Dough Charm

To make this bread clay use leftover slices of bread from the Lughnasadh bread recipe in this section. If you need to you can substitute plain white bread for the herbed Lughnasadh bread, and simply add loose dried herbs to the clay.

Materials:
White craft glue
Herbed Lughnasadh Bread - ripped into chunks
Lemon juice

Tools:
Mixing bowl
4 tbsp white craft glue
4 slices white bread without the crusts
2 tsp Lemon juice

Tear up the bread into small pieces. In a bowl mix together the bread, glue, and lemon juice. If you need to, add more dry herbs at this time. You can select herbs from the correspondence list for this Sabbat or just choose some that you like.

Stir the contents together thoroughly; as it starts to stick together knead it with your hands. Knead the clay until smooth. Form a rough rock shape with the dough and use an empty ball point pen to carve magick symbols and shapes into the rock.

Consider your wishes for the coming year. Ask for prosperity, peace and good health for yourself and your loved ones. Give thanks for all that you have already. Bake your rock in the oven on a cookie sheet at the lowest setting until dry. This can take as long as a few hours so check it frequently and when it is hard and slightly golden you can remove it.

Your herbed rock will smell wonderful as it bakes. Place the cooled rock on your Lughnasadh altar.

Lughnasadh Corn Stalks

Make huge cornstalks out of recycled newspaper to decorate your house during the season.

Tape several sheets of newspaper together lengthwise. Roll the newspaper up lengthwise. Tape the end closed. Use scissors to cut several slits in one end of the newspaper roll. With your fingers pull out the center of the newspaper roll. Watch it grow longer. The flaps of newspaper will fall over to resemble corn stalk leaves of sheaves of wheat.

You can paint the newspaper to look like cornstalks or wheat.

Lughnasadh Recipe - Lammas Bread

Herbed Lughnasadh bread is a wonderful treat to celebrate this first harvest.

2 tsps garlic powder
2 tsps onion powder
2 tsps dried basil
2 tsps dried dill weed
2 tbsps dried parsley
1 cup warm water
3 tbsp sugar
2 packets of yeast
3 tbsp olive oil
1 cup milk
1 tsp salt
6-7 cups flour
2 large mixing bowls, one greased
dish towel
2 greased bread loaf pans

Dried herbs need to be crushed to better release their flavor and fragrance. You can crush your herbs with a mortar in pestle, or use a spoon to crush them in a small bowl.

In a large mixing bowl pour 1 cup of warm water. Stir in 1 tbsp sugar and sprinkle 2 packets of yeast on top. Let the yeast sit for about five minutes. When it is ready it will look frothy.

To this bowl add 3 tbsp of olive oil, 1 cup milk, 1 tsp salt, all of the dried herbs, and the remaining 2 tbsp of sugar. Mix this up well. Add 3 cups of flour to the bowl and stir vigorously. Stir the batter clockwise, and counter-clockwise. Pagans some times call clockwise, widdershins, and counter-clockwise deosil (pronounced jesl). Practice saying these words as you stir.

As you stir. the batter will start turning into a stringy dough at this point. Add another three or four cups of flour to the batter. Keep stirring the dough, it will be difficult to stir at this point and the dough will start to form a ball and pull away from the sides of the bowl. Remove the dough from the bowl and place it on a floured surface.

Knead the dough with your hands and work in more flour if it feels too sticky. To knead pull and stretch the dough with your hands and push it back onto itself. You can flatten the dough out and fold it over, then turn it and repeat this step of flattening and folding. Knead the dough for about 5-10 minutes.

Pat the dough into a ball and place it in the greased bowl. Turn the dough in the bowl a bit to cover its surface with a little bit of oil. Cover the dough with a dish towel. Allow the dough to sit in a warm place for about an hour. When you check on the dough it should have expanded to about twice its original size!

Now comes the fun part. Make a fist and punch the middle of the dough to deflate it. This is fine; you want the dough to deflate so that it can rise again. Cover the dough and allow it to rise to twice its size once more. This may take about 20-30 minutes.

Remove the dough from the bowl and pinch off a section about the size of an adult fist. Then divide the remaining dough in half. Let this rest for about 10 minutes.

Take one of the two large sections of dough and make it into a loaf shape. Place it in the greased loaf pan.

Cut off half of the smaller dough ball you set aside. Use this to make decorative pieces for the top of your loaf. You can cut out shapes with cookies cutters or make stalks of wheat to decorate the top of your harvest loaf.

To make the deocrations roll three snakes of dough. Make small angled cuts in one end of the snake. The cuts should travel to only about 1/3 of the way up the stalk. Arrange these three wheat stalks on top of the bread loaf. Use several small snakes of dough to make a ribbon to press over the wheat stalks. Repeat this with the other section of dough so that you have two loaves of bread ready to be baked.

Let the dough rise in the loaf pans. Bake the loaves in the oven at 425 degrees for about 25 to 30 minutes. The loaves will be done when they are lightly golden and make a hollow sound when the top is tapped.

Take the loaves out of the oven brush the tops with melted butter. Allow the loaves to cool for at least 30 minutes before slicing them; otherwise, they will be doughy.

Enjoy your harvest bread and don't forget to save a few slices for making your harvest bread clay.

Apple Pentacle Stamps

Did you know that if you cut an apple in half through it's middle that you will see a pentacle in the cross section? A pentacle is a five pointed star surrounded by a circle. It represents the four earthly elements and the fifth element of spirit.

You can make stamps from apples but cutting them in half widthwise for a pentacle shape in lengthwise for an apple shape. Have an adult cut the apples for you. Then use a disposable plate to hold a few dollops of craft paint. You can apply the paint to your apply with a brush or dip it directly in the paint (if you dip the apple you may need to blot it a bit with a paper towel before stamping your project).

Make an apple wreath by stamping the apples in a circle pattern on a large piece of paper. Stamp a single imprint on the center of a blank card for Lughnasadh Sabbat cards. Use fabric paint to make a Lughnasadh t-shirt, tote bag, and baseball cap or hand towel. Cut out stamp prints and glue them around a strip of paper to make an apple crown. Use your imagination!

Dream Pillow

Make a dream pillow to help you sleep soundly and encourage lovely and prophetic dreams. The instructions for this craft use fabric glue so that young children can make a pillow. If you prefer to machine or hand sew the pillow you can do so with the help of an adult.

Tools and supplies:
Decorative fabric
Fabric Glue
½ cup Lavender
½ cup Sage
Poly fiberfill for stuffing pillows
Clothespins or clips

Cut two rectangles from your fabric. 9x 12 is a good size. Stack the fabric wrong sides together. Remove the top piece of fabric and set it to the side. Squeeze a line of glue around the edges of the fabric, about ½ inch from the edge. Run the glue along three sides of the fabric and halfway across the fourth side. Press the top piece of
fabric down onto the bottom piece. Let the glue dry.

Turn the pillowcase right side out. Fill the pillow halfway up with poly fiberfill. Then pour in ½ cup of lavender and ½ cup of sage. Fill the pillow the rest of the way with more fiberfill. Glue the opening of the pillow shut and hold it closed with clothespins (or another kind of clip) while it dries.

Place the dream pillow under your real pillow and breathe in its scent. Pleasant dreams!

Oatmeal Soap Ball

Make this oatmeal soap ball and get squeaky clean for your Sabbat celebration

Tools and Supplies:
½ cup oatmeal
½ cup grated bar soap
1 tbsp olive oil
1 tbsp water

Grate a soap bar of your choice using a cheese grater. In a bowl mix together all of the ingredients with your hands. Mush the soap around with your hands and form it into a ball. If it is too dry add a little more olive oil, water or both. When you have a satisfactory ball shape set the soap ball on a piece of wax paper and allow it to dry for about 24 hours. It should be firm and not too sticky to the touch when it is dry. Now scrub away your troubles with a bath of oatmeal bubbles!

LUGHNASADH

LUGHNASADH
Word Search

J	O	H	N	B	A	R	L	E	Y	C	O	R	N
V	C	T	I	C	D	A	L	U	G	H	D	C	P
K	E	I	A	N	M	F	E	K	P	T	P	E	S
P	Q	G	U	C	S	D	W	E	H	A	F	E	Y
V	E	O	E	F	M	A	U	G	U	S	T	Y	L
W	H	E	A	T	X	E	P	A	K	H	A	D	L
C	Q	S	N	H	A	R	V	E	S	T	B	G	O
E	X	E	C	S	U	B	O	P	N	E	B	N	D
G	R	A	I	N	P	E	L	S	I	N	A	I	N
C	A	E	B	M	A	S	A	E	I	A	T	K	R
I	S	Y	S	T	U	O	R	P	S	I	B	A	O
C	O	R	N	A	I	N	S	X	G	T	E	B	C

HARVEST   LUGH
CORN DOLLY   GRAIN
WHEAT   VEGETABLES
CORN   JOHN BARLEYCORN
BREAD   SPROUTS
AUGUST   BAKING

NOTES

NOTES

NOTES

NOTES

NOTES

NOTES

NOTES

NOTES

Mabon

Chapter Eight

Fall – Mabon

Other Names: Autumnal Equinox, Me'an Fo'mhair, Alban Elfed, Second Harvest Festival, Wine Harvest, Grape Harvest, Feast of Avalon, Cornucopia
Northern Hemisphere: September 20-23
Southern Hemisphere: March 20-23
Herbs: Acorn, ferns, grains, honeysuckle, marigold, rose, sage.
Incense: cinnamon, apple, marigold, myrrh, sage
Colors: Gold, Yellow, orange, red, brown, purple, dark blue
Decorations: horns of plenty, gourds, pine cones, acorns, corn, apples, seeds
Foods: grape juice, apples, grains, vegetables, squash, pumpkin pie, corn.
Gods: Mabon, Father Sky, Thoth, Thor, Hermes, The Green Man
Goddesses: Mother Earth, Morgaine, Epona, Persephone
Spirit: Thanksgiving, charity, compassion, family, remembrance, harmony, peace, balance

Mabon is a time of thanksgiving, not unlike the national holidays of Thanksgiving found in a number of countries. It is the Autumnal Equinox and like Ostara is a Sabbat based on balance and harmony. The Sun again crosses the Celestial Equator, and we have a day and night of equal length.

Mabon is a time of reflection, remembrance and preparation for the dark half of the year. The Earth is moving into winter for its long slumber. Traditionally ancient people were harvesting and storing food at this time for the long winter ahead. Most holidays involve spending time with family, but at Mabon especially we should give thanks for our loved ones and good fortune in our lives.

Mabon Altar

The Mabon altar is full of the colors of autumn. Go outside and gather acorns, pinecones, fall leaves and sticks for your altar.

Trace fall leaves onto construction paper, cut out the leaves, punch a hole in them and thread them on ribbon to make garlands of fall colors for all over your home.

Glue leaves to a paper plate with the center cut out to make a fall wreath. To make a placemat gather fall leaves and arrange them on a sheet of wax paper. Use a pencil sharpener to shave wax off of some crayons. Put the crayon wax on the wax paper, cover with another sheet and have an adult iron the piece at a low setting.

Place a towel over the wax paper to protect the iron. The wax will melt and hold the sheets together. Trim the edges and place this on your altar or use it to decorate your thanksgiving table.

Mabon Ritual – Pine Cone Bird Feeder

This craft is an excellent way to give thanks to Mother nature and her creatures. Gather pinecones from outside. Tie yarn to the top of the cones to make hanging loops. Coat the cones with peanut butter. Really mush the peanut butter down into the grooves between the spikes on the pinecone. Then roll the pinecone in birdseed.

Gather your family together and go outside. Hang the pinecone bird feeders on some trees. You can do this in your backyard or a local park. Have every family member take a moment and share something that they are thankful for. Take your time and really think about the blessings in your life.

We all have times when it may be hard to figure out what we are thankful for, especially if we are going through a difficult period in our lives. But generally we can all find at least a little something to be thankful for.

Just look at the birds enjoying your bird feeder. Now that is a lovely thing, and the birds are thankful you made it!

Mabon Recipe – Equinox Cookies

These easy to make cookies represent the balanced qualities of the holiday.
1 box vanilla wafers
1 bag chocolate chips
1 bag white chocolate chips

Melt a small bowl of chocolate chips in the microwave. They melt quickly so heat them for only about 20 seconds at a time until they are melted. Cover a cookie sheet with wax paper. Dip each vanilla wafer halfway into the chocolate and set it carefully on the wax paper to cool. When the cookies are cool and the chocolate is set, melt a small bowl of white chocolate chips in the microwave. Dip the uncoated halves of the cookies in the white chocolate. Lay the cookies on the wax paper to cool. Serve and enjoy these sweets that represent the balance of light and darkness.

Baker's Clay Cornucopia

Cornucopia literally means Horn of Plenty. It is a traditional symbol of prosperity and bounty. The Cornucopia is shaped looks like a horn shaped basket and is generally shown overflowing with fruits, nuts, and vegetables. It comes from a story about the God Zeus who as a baby plucked a horn from the head of a goat and gave it the ability to overflow with whatever its owner desired. It has become a popular symbol used at Thanksgiving and certainly is appropriate at Mabon.

3 1/2 cups flour
1 cup salt
1 1/4 - 1 1/2 cup water

Cardboard
Aluminum foil
rolling pin

Mix the flour and salt together in a bowl. Add the water slowly and continue stirring. You want the consistency of clay, not to dry, not too sticky. You may need to add more or less water to get the desired texture.

Depending on the size of Cornucopia you are going to make you may need to double or triple this recipe. You may want to start out small. You can always make a large size later. Make a cone shaped frame out of a piece of cardboard. Bend the cardboard into a cone shape and secure it with a stapler. Cover the cone with aluminum foil. Make a free form shape out of foil to serve as the end of the horn. Press it onto the cone.

Roll out the baker's clay on a sheet of wax paper. Completely cover the cardboard frame with baker's clay. Smooth all the seams together. Roll snakes of clay and braid three together, press this braid around the opening edge of the horn. You can make other braids to decorate the rest of the horn.

Cut shapes out with cookies cutters or carve designs into the horn. To make the surface of the horn brown to a golden color you can beat an egg white with a tsp of water and brush this mixture on the horn. To bake the dough set it in the oven on a cookie sheet at 300 degrees for about an hour. Turn the horn periodically and brush on more egg white mixture. After an hour remove your cardboard frame and bake the horn for another 15 minutes or so. Do not allow it to burn.

When the horn is cool you can have an adult spray it with a clear protective coating such as acrylic spray or polyurethane.

Fill your horn with real or fake fruits, veggies, and nuts. It makes a great decoration for the dinner table.

Autumn Poncho

Make a warm poncho for autumn from fleece fabric.

Tools and Supplies:
1-3 yards of fleece fabric (depending on your height)
Scissors
Puffy Fabric Paint
Fabric Glue
Assorted colors of scrap felt or fleece
Embroidery floss and needle (optional)

To make this poncho you will need to measure the length of your arms from one wrist, up across your shoulders to the next wrist. You will need a square piece of fabric cut to this measurement. Turn the square on the diagonal so that it is in a diamond shape. Cut a vertical slit in the center of the fabric about six inches long. Try and fit the poncho over your head. If you need to, cut the slit a little bigger until you can easily fit the poncho over your head, yet it doesn't sag off your shoulders. If you use a fabric such as fleece or felt you won't have to hem any edges. Cut shapes and designs from more fabric and glue them to your poncho with fabric glue. Use puffy fabric paints to draw designs (paint on paints won't show up through the fibers of these fabrics) If you are adept with a needle and thread you can use embroidery floss and a needle to create more designs.

Polymer Clay Cauldron

Build a polymer clay cauldron to use for decoration during Samhain. When using polymer clay it is best to purchase an inexpensive toaster oven for baking the clay and use this little oven exclusively for craft projects. Polymer clay is non-toxic but the clay residue can build up in your kitchen oven and could be potentially unhealthy. Better to be safe then sorry.

Materials:
Toaster oven
Black polymer clay
pencil
Pipe cleaners

Roll a long snake of clay and coil it up onto itself to make a stacked spiral shape. Smooth the sides of the clay together to form a cauldron belly. Form legs and poke two holes with a pencil near the top edge of the cauldron to later attach a handle. Bake in the toaster oven according to the manufacturer's directions. You can have an adult carefully drop the cauldron into a large bowl of ice water to cool it off quicker. Fashion a handle from pipe cleaners.

Autumn Weaving Wall Hanging

You will make this wall hanging almost entirely from mother nature's materials!
Gather three sticks of about equal size and length. Bind the three sticks together in the shape of a triangle.
Bind the sticks together with strong twine and tie secure knots. Using more twine or string wind across the framework randomly. Wind the string around the sticks and across to the next. Cover the framework very well, breaking up any empty space.

Gather leaves, feathers, acorns, dried flowers, and herbs from outside. If you have any recycled objects or other craft supplies you would like to use, gather those as well. Tuck the leaves and feathers in between the strings of your weaving.

Use craft glue to glue on bits of dried grasses and acorns. Hang bunches of dried herbs from colorful ribbon. Your weaving should be a wild explosion of autumn.

Make a hanging loop and decorate an empty wall!

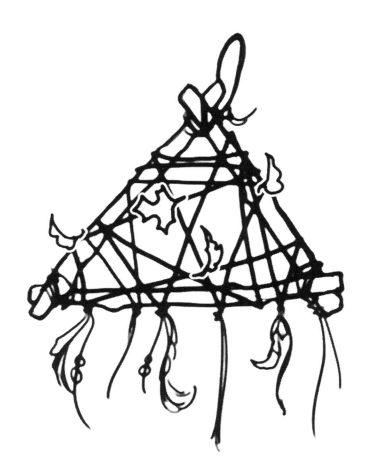

Prayer Flag

In Tibet they have a traditional religious object called a prayer flag. Sometimes these prayer flags are a single piece of cloth or several pieces attached to a long string. Prayers and requests are written on the prayer flags and hung outside to be carried to the Gods in the crisp breeze. Autumn can be a very blustery time of year, and what a great season to make a prayer flag.

To make your prayer flag you will need five plain rectangles of fabric. You can use old scraps in any color you like. You will need to be able to write on the fabric so avoid felt or anything with a nap, smooth fabric will work best. Glue the tops of your flags to a long piece of ribbon with fabric or craft glue. Don't worry about hemming the fabric, it will take a beating in the wind and start to unravel regardless.

Use a black permanent marker to write your prayers, requests, wishes and desires, for yourself, your loved ones, or your country onto the flags. If you wish you can use a secret alphabet to keep your prayer personal. You can use the rune writing alphabet or make up your own code that only you know. Draw symbols and pictures representing your prayer request on the flags.

Hang the flag line outside so that it can dance in the breeze without laying on the ground. Watch your prayers being carried on the wind!

MABON

MABON
Word Search

G	R	A	P	E	H	A	R	V	E	S	T	G	F
R	T	U	O	S	D	R	U	O	G	O	W	N	E
A	I	N	E	U	B	R	N	T	C	S	A	P	A
P	M	A	U	C	L	I	A	N	U	R	O	C	S
E	O	G	I	M	A	B	O	N	P	M	N	F	T
J	Q	O	A	T	K	R	E	K	V	H	N	A	R
U	L	U	S	C	D	A	E	R	B	N	R	O	C
I	N	D	I	A	I	N	S	V	S	R	K	X	G
C	N	E	S	N	R	O	C	A	G	B	A	S	L
E	D	H	R	G	O	I	E	S	E	V	A	E	L
W	S	T	B	G	C	X	H	Y	K	S	Y	I	A
S	E	P	T	E	M	B	E	R	Q	G	N	A	F

MABON   GOURDS
AUTUMN   FEAST
EQUINOX   SEPTEMBER
GRAPE HARVEST   FALL
CORN BREAD   LEAVES
ACORNS   GRAPE JUICE

NOTES

NOTES

NOTES

NOTES

NOTES

NOTES

Samhain

Chapter Nine

Fall/Winter - Samhain

Other Names: Third Harvest, Day of the Dead, Old Hallowmas, Shadowfest, All Hallow's Eve, Martinmas, Witch's New Year, Halloween.
Northern Hemisphere: October 31st November 1
Southern Hemisphere: April 30 -May 1
Herbs: Mugwort, Allspice, Broom, Catnip, Oak leaves, Sage, Straw, Rosemary, sunflower, pumpkin seeds, pine needles, garlic
Incense: cinnamon, sage, mint, nutmeg, rosemary
Colors: black, orange, white, silver, gold, brown, rust
Decorations: gourds, apples, cats, Jack-O-Lanterns, brooms, pumpkins.
Foods: apples, nuts, cider, squash, corn, soup, pumpkin
Gods: Herne, The Hunter, Anubis, The Sage
Goddesses: The Crone, Hecate
Spirit: Family, remembrance of the dead, introspection

Samhain is sometimes celebrated as the Pagan New Year. It is considered a night when the veil between the world of the living and the world of the dead is thinnest. This doesn't have to be a scary thing. In fact there are many Samhain traditions that are a lovely way of remembering those we love that have passed on. Some families set a dinner plate at the table for every loved one that has passed over. They set out pictures and photos albums of them and tell stories remembering the one's they miss.

This holiday, much like Yule, is a great time for resolutions. Write down what you hope to accomplish in the new year and put it in a bowl on your Samhain altar. Afterwards keep the slip of paper in a safe place, check it often to remind yourself of your goals.

Samhain is a wonderful Sabbat in it's own right, but perhaps is even more popular because of it's close association with Halloween. Many Pagans celebrate both holidays. Some have separate celebrations for each, dividing the serious topics from the lighthearted; others incorporate the two together for a fun and inspiring celebration. Whatever you choose I hope you have a fun and safe time.

Enjoy yourself by decorating and making costumes but don't neglect to consider the more serious side of Samhain, and take a moment to remember those who have gone before. Even if you have not lost anyone close to you, we can all find brave and worthy people throughout history and in our local communities who deserve a moment of quiet remembrance in honor of their good works.

Samhain Altar

Wow! The Samhain altar is an altar bursting with texture and color. For this holiday you may want to drag out the full altar set up. If you have a cauldron display it proudly. Fill it with candy, or floating candles. Drape rich fabrics in gold and black across your table. Prints with stars and moons echo the dark decoration of the Samhain night sky. Witches on brooms are no stranger to Halloween decorations, but maybe you can draw a portrait of one you know personally and display them at your table. Set up framed pictures of loved ones, living and deceased. Pumpkins, and gourds make great decorations. Carve a pumpkin in a fabulous design and set them up indoors as well as out. Sprinkle flour around to give your table a dusty spooky look, and set your broom up in the corner.

Samhain Ritual – Remembrance Dinner

If you have lost a loved one in your life, whether it be a friend, relative or pet, you may appreciate the quiet enjoyment of a remembrance dinner. There are a few ways to go about this, and your family should choose the tone that suits your personalities best. A common theme at a remembrance dinner or feast of the dead, is to set a place setting at the table for those people (or pets) you wish to honor. Some people prefer a solemn supper, with no speaking, just quiet reflection on those who have passed while they eat their meal. Other people prefer a boisterous occasion with festive spooky food and lots of conversation. There is not right or wrong, just do whatever suits your family.

Solemn Feast – Fix favorite dishes of the deceased loved ones. Set a formal dinner table and put pictures of those passed at their place settings. Dress in formal attire and arrive at the table at a set time. Eat in silence and quietly consider those you have lost. Afterwards share your thoughts with your family. Flip through photo albums and tell anecdotes.

Boisterous Feast – Fix festive Halloween gag food, such as spaghetti with eyeballs (cut an olive in half and insert it in a meatball). Spider shaped dinner rolls (fashion a body from refrigerated crescent dough, roll long legs and press to the body) and Ice Scream (ice cream with strawberry sauce and gummy bugs). Draw pictures of your loved ones who have passed, and make lists of funny things they did to share with everyone at the table. Watch funny videos, drink punch and cause a ruckus. No one leaves the table till someone falls off their chair from laughing too hard!

Samhain Recipe – Pumpkin Bread

Make a delicious bread to share from one of the best treats of the season!
3 cups canned pumpkin
1 1/2 cups vegetable oil
4 cups sugar
6 eggs
4 3/4 cups flour (all-purpose)
1 1/2 tsps baking powder
1 1/2 tsps baking soda
1 1/2 tsps salt
1 1/2 tsps cinnamon
2 regular size bread loaf pans or muffin tins with muffin cup liners.

Have an adult preheat your oven to 350 degrees. Grease your bread loaf pans or spray them with oil spray. In a large bowl mix the pumpkin, sugar, eggs, and oil together. In another bowl combine the flour, baking soda, salt, and cinnamon. Stir this mixture into the pumpkin mixture bowl and stir everything well. Pour the batter into the two loaf pans being sure to divide it up evenly. Bake the loaves for about 45 minutes to an hour and have an adult check them to see when they are done. If you are making muffins you will bake them for only 30 minutes. You can add raisins, nuts, chocolate chips or white chocolate chips to your loaves if you like. Wrap your loaves in plastic wrap to store them.

Halloween Slime

Yucky slime to gross out your friends
Tools and Supplies:
1 cup white craft glue
¾ cup water
1 tbsp craft paint, any color
Borax

Mix the glue, water and paint together with a plastic spoon. In a separate bowl mix together about 1/3 cup of water and ½ tsp of borax. Pour the dissolved borax into the bowl with the glue mixture.
Let the mixture set for a few minutes, then knead it with your hands. Pour out the water and store the slime in plastic baggies or containers.

Magic Potion

You can make this magic potion in your cauldron or a plastic container.

Materials:
Baking soda
Vinegar
Food coloring
Rectangular cake pan

Set your cauldron or container into the cake pan. In your cauldron dissolve 2 tbsp of water, 1 tbsp baking soda, and a few drops of food coloring. Be sure the baking soda is dissolved. In a small cup pour 2 tbsps of vinegar. Wave your hand over the cauldron and shout, Bubbleus Majorus! and in one swift flourish dump the entire contents of the cup into the cauldron. Your magic potion will bubble and froth and flow over the sides of the cauldron.

Magickal Besom

A besom is another word for a broom. Make your very own magickal broom. Use it for exploring your backyard, winning that big game of Quidditch, or tidying up the kitchen!

Materials:
1 store bought household broom
craft paints
metallic paint pens
craft glue

Tools:
sandpaper

Embellishments:
charms
silk flowers
beads
glitter spray
glitter
ribbons
stickers
stamps

Sand the handle of your broom a bit to get the shine off of it. This will allow the paint to adhere better to the handle. Decorate the handle of your broom with paints, stickers, glitter and magickal symbols. Tie ribbon around the base of the broom. Add herbs or silk flowers if you wish. String beads and charms onto the ends of the ribbons. Use glitter spray to give the broom bristles a sparkle. Hop on and give it a twirl. Who knows, maybe you will be the player on your Quidditch team! :)

Polymer Clay Cauldron

Build a polymer clay cauldron to use for decoration during Samhain. When using polymer clay it is best to purchase an inexpensive toaster oven for baking the clay and use this little oven exclusively for craft projects. Polymer clay is non-toxic but the clay residue can build up in your kitchen oven and could be potentially unhealthy. Better to be safe then sorry.

Materials:
Toaster oven
Black polymer clay
pencil
Pipe cleaners

Roll a long snake of clay and coil it up onto itself to make a stacked spiral shape. Smooth the sides of the clay together to form a cauldron belly. Form legs and poke two holes with a pencil near the top edge of the cauldron to later attach a handle. Bake in the toaster oven according to the manufacturer's directions. You can have an adult carefully drop the cauldron into a large bowl of ice water to cool it off quicker. Fashion a handle from pipe cleaners. Alternatively you can smooth a sheet of polymer clay about ¼ inch thick onto a small oven safe bowl. Poke the handle holes in the sides, and attach legs to the bottom of the cauldron. Bake it upside down supported by the bowl.

SAMHAIN

SAMHAIN
Word Search

H	Y	I	A	B	R	O	O	M	D	N	C	T
S	A	M	H	A	I	N	C	T	I	C	D	S
I	Q	L	F	O	P	D	R	O	B	P	A	E
C	Y	U	L	C	A	U	L	D	R	O	N	V
A	E	G	A	O	E	B	R	S	W	E	E	R
N	K	P	T	S	W	E	O	A	G	I	W	A
D	N	S	I	T	H	E	U	X	E	S	Y	H
Y	N	C	S	U	B	H	E	A	T	L	E	T
E	D	P	U	M	P	K	I	N	Y	C	A	S
C	A	P	S	E	U	G	L	O	H	A	R	A
J	A	C	K	O	L	A	N	T	E	R	N	L
C	T	E	B	S	R	O	T	S	E	C	N	A

SAMHAIN   PUMPKIN
HALLOWEEN   SQUASH
COSTUME   LAST HARVEST
CAULDRON   JACK O LANTERN
NEW YEAR   BROOM
ANCESTORS   CANDY

NOTES

NOTES

NOTES

NOTES

NOTES

NOTES

NOTES

NOTES

WORD SEARCH GUIDE

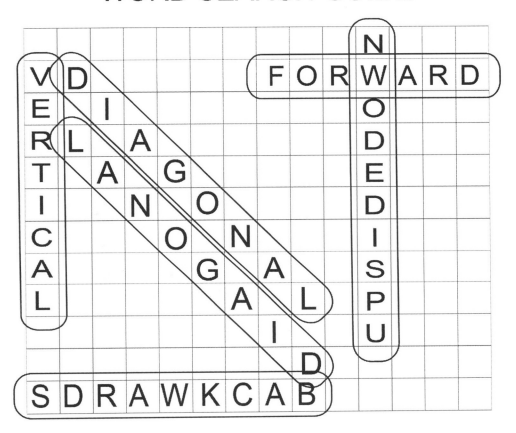

VERTICAL
DIAGONAL (X2)
BACKWARDS
FORWARD
UPSIDE DOWN